Build a Classic
Timber-Framed House

- Planning and Design
- Traditional Materials
- Affordable Methods

By Jack A. Sobon

*All drawings and photographs by the author
unless otherwise noted*

A Garden Way Publishing Book

STOREY

STOREY COMMUNICATIONS, INC.

SCHOOLHOUSE ROAD

POWNAL, VERMONT 05261

Front cover frame photograph by A. Blake Gardner, back cover photograph and finished house front cover photograph by Martha Storey
Edited by John Matthews, Wood-Matthews Editorial Services, Inc.
Cover and text design by Cindy McFarland
Text production by Cindy McFarland and Susan Bernier
Indexed by Jeremy Seeger

The information in this book is true and complete to the best of our knowledge. All recommendations are made without guarantee on the part of the author or Storey Communications, Inc. The author and publisher disclaim any liability in connection with the use of this information. For additional information, please contact Storey Communications, Inc., Schoolhouse Road, Pownal, Vermont 05261.

Garden Way Publishing was founded in 1973 as part of the Garden Way Incorporated Group of Companies, dedicated to bringing gardening information and equipment to as many people as possible. Today the name "Garden Way Publishing" is licensed to Storey Communications, Inc., in Pownal, Vermont. For a complete list of Garden Way Publishing titles, call 1-800-827-8673. Garden Way Incorporated manufactures products in Troy, New York, under the Troy-Bilt® brand including garden tillers, chipper/shredders, mulching mowers, sicklebar mowers, and tractors. For information on any Garden Way Incorporated product, please call 1-800-345-4454.

Printed in the United States by Book Press
First Printing, December 1993

Library of Congress Cataloging-in-Publication Data

Sobon, Jack, 1955–
    Build a classic timber-framed house : planning and design : traditional methods : affordable methods / by Jack A. Sobon ; all drawings and photographs by the author unless otherwise noted.
        p.   cm.
    "A Garden Way Publishing book."
    Includes bibliographical references (p.   ) and index.
    ISBN 0-88266-842-0 (hc) — ISBN 0-88266-841-2 (pbk.)
    1. Wooden-frame houses—Design and construction—Amateurs' manuals.   I. Title.
TH4818.W6S62   1994
694—dc20   93-14118
                       CIP

Contents

Acknowledgments

I would like to thank Jay and Vicki Dwight, the owners of our project
house, for allowing me to draw upon the building of their
timber-framed house.

◆

I would also like to thank Dave Bowman and Steve Westcott for their help
in cutting the timber joinery and erecting the frame.

◆

Lastly, I want to thank my wife, Susan, and my daughters, Larissa and
Hannah, for bearing with me during the writing of this book.

Introduction

This is a book about building a traditional timber-framed house. This book is not a romantic retrospective to see how things were done in the "good old days" — it describes practical methods to enable you to build your own timber-framed home. I show how to build with local, inexpensive materials and your own labor to create a house that is healthy for its occupants and our planet, a house that can endure, build community spirit, and be easily expanded to accommodate changing needs. The low-tech approach presented here also makes this house affordable.

When the timber-framing revival began in the 1970s, some builders attempted to bring back some of the things we had lost through the rapid advance of technology. People became involved with the building of their own houses, and some resurrected community house raisings and the use of local materials. Houses began to be sited again to take advantage of natural systems. Unfortunately, timber framing itself has become high-tech in the last 20 years. With all the trappings of high-tech house building, timber framing is financially beyond the reach of most people. And with noxious materials used in construction and walls that don't breathe, many so-called state-of-the-art houses are not healthy.

Most of today's houses use materials that are too expensive for the owner-builder. Homes are becoming like automobiles: factory-produced plugged-in modules. Industry is taking over the

▲ *Old buildings have a story to tell, but it takes a bit of timber-frame detective work to uncover it.*

craftsperson's realm. Even the tools of timber framing have changed since the 1970s: Very expensive power tools have become the norm in many timber-framing shops, and a person contemplating building a timber-framed house can be easily discouraged by the price of these tools alone. But you needn't spend money on such tools. I will show you how hand tools can save you money and bring back the dignity of the craft.

Most owner-builders are not architects or engineers, yet a good design is essential to a successful home. Many owner-builders have been led to believe that timber-frame structural design — the

sizing of beams and spans, for example — is a simple process that can be mastered as easily as stud framing with the aid of some tables and charts. Unfortunately, timber framing is much more complex, and there are no appropriate tables or readily available resources for the owner-builder to construct a structurally sound home (see Appendix A). This book presents a classic house design that has been with us for over three hundred years and is simple and affordable and has noble proportions. Although modest in size, you can easily expand or adapt the design — its timber framing is straightforward but strong. You don't need to be

BUILD A CLASSIC TIMBER-FRAMED HOUSE

a design professional because most of the design work has been done for you.

In the following pages, we first look at the timber-framing tradition as it was originally practiced. The history of timber framing is important to understand because the social and economic factors that guided the development of the craft are becoming important again today. A building craft that used minimally processed local raw materials and hand labor created houses that were affordable, attractive, healthy, and durable with materials that were recyclable and biodegradable. With increasing energy costs and the effects of buildings on our health

becoming better known, many people are beginning to realize that the old traditions are desirable and may even be necessary for our culture to survive.

After examining the relevant history of timber framing, we will look at design considerations, such as the best way to heat and light the house. How can the house be integrated with its site? How can we best take advantage of natural forces?

You will then learn about selecting timber and how to use trees on your own property for timbers, planks, and boards. The layout and cutting of the timber-frame joinery are covered in detail along

▲ *This house in western Massachusetts was our project house. It combines classic good looks with economy and flexibility.*

▲ *Part of the allure of this old system of building is that the owner can take an active role in home building.*

with sections on making pegs and on selecting and sharpening tools, and I will guide you through the frame assembly and raising sequence. Remember that a community house raising makes the most sense for this frame — Is there a better way for a house to begin its life?

A timber frame is only a skeleton, so I also describe how to complete the house. All aspects of construction unique to a timber-framed house are discussed in some detail. This book is not encumbered with all the nitty-gritty details that are found in conventional house building books, however: You won't read about

how to flash a chimney, install a doorknob, or paint a window. I do include references to other resources — books, magazines, tools, and companies — offering up-to-date information.

Finally, I show that the design can be modified to suit your specific needs and can be enlarged in a multitude of ways to grow with you over the years. Starting with a modest house means a modest mortgage. The size of the design can even be shrunk to become a woods cabin, workshop, or office. The flexibility of this house design is one of the reasons it has been used for several centuries. Some of you may also be concerned with self-sufficiency, so we also look at how this house can be part of a larger homestead.

I hope that this book will make timber-framed homes available to more people than ever before. If you have some land, some time, and the desire to build, this book will help you create a strong, handsome, and enduring timber-framed house.

Jack A. Sobon
Windsor, Massachusetts
September 1993

CHAPTER 1

Building on the Past

What Used to Be

Before we can begin building, we must first understand and look at traditional timber-framed home building to see what we can use and how we might improve on what we find. Before the Industrial Revolution, the craft of building concerned itself with raw materials; with human-, animal-, water-, and wind-powered processes; and with tradition and integrity. Building was a business, but it was a humane business. Your builder lived locally and simply had to do quality work.

Your builder knew the language of building, which determined the layout, material usage, and the construction details. There is little or no language in much of today's building — anyone with a pickup truck and a circular saw can be a builder. This book is an attempt to reintroduce some of the lost building language of timber-framed houses.

In the past, the materials — stone and timber — were often taken from the local forest or quarry and incorporated into the building with a minimum of processing

▲ *Before the days of transit-mixed concrete, local stone was used for foundations, which provided ample work for local masons. This old mill foundation of dry-laid stone has not fallen after decades without a roof.*

▲ *After two hundred years, this Cape Cod–style house was dismantled and relocated. Will today's houses be worthy of salvage someday?*

and handling. The builder knew how the stone and timber should be worked and used to their best advantage and the lifespan, strengths, and weaknesses of these materials. Who can claim such a knowledge of twentieth-century materials? If a building was ravaged by fire or storm or suffered from neglect and became unusable, there wasn't a disposal problem: no pollution, no problems. Doesn't this make sense again today? What will disposing of today's homes and their nonbiodegradable materials cost us?

Old builders sited and oriented their houses to take the best advantage of natural systems. Sun, prevailing winds, groundwater, soils, vegetation, and drainage were all considered since great amounts of energy are necessary to alter or compensate for site deficiencies. Because buildings had to work with their environment, they were naturally comfortable with their site, making the occupants more comfortable inside. When fossil fuels became prevalent, we began to build in spite of natural systems; in fact,

we often ignored them. We are now at a turning point where we must go back to the older, more intelligent way. We no longer have the energy or resources to continue on our current path.

Today, when we speak of buildings that use local materials, local builders, and local traditions, we use the term *vernacular architecture*. Tepees, igloos, adobe houses, English timbered buildings, and Norwegian log structures are all examples of vernacular buildings. In a given area, vernacular buildings are the most economical and the most suited to the culture and climate and, in general, make the most sense for that area. When a building anywhere in the world looks friendly, inviting, and at peace with its environment, it is likely that it is a vernacular building. Lately, there has been a resurgence in the study and revival of vernacular building traditions worldwide. The hall-and-parlor house discussed in this book continues the vernacular tradition of much of the eastern United States.

Preindustrial buildings also had romance. Romance is not just something we feel now as we look back — old systems of building even appear to have been romantic in the past. When you combine nature's materials, a lot of handwork, and the ancient traditions of building, you get a building that can really mean something to its owner.

It is precisely romance that prompted the revival of the timber-framed building tradition here in the 1970s. The industrial age had removed most of the romance and craft from building to make life easier for humankind. Some saw the inadequacies of the building industry and, through timber framing, log building, adobe, and other local building methods, people began reviving vernacular traditions. An important change had occurred: The process of building became as important as the end product.

What Is Timber Framing?

Before looking at a brief history of the craft, it is necessary to define timber framing: Timber framing is a traditional building system that uses a skeletal framework of both large and small wooden members fastened to each other with joinery. Principal members may be joined with elaborate mortise-and-tenon joints and locked with wooden pins, whereas some nonstructural joints may be butted together and anchored with iron spikes. Iron nails, straps, and bolts are invariably found in the best of the old timber-framed structures, but at least some of the structural connections rely on wooden joinery. Simply stacking beams on top of posts and fastening them with metal hardware is not timber framing but, rather, post-and-beam construction. Although Europe most often comes to mind when we think of the evolution of timber framing, equally fine traditions of the craft exist in the Far East.

A History of Timber Framing

The craft probably began soon after humans began to use tools to work wood. The use of the mortise-and-tenon joint is at least three thousand years old, as the furniture found in King Tutankhamen's tomb attests, and all of the oldest surviving timber-framed buildings indicate that the craft was already at an advanced state when they were built. We may never understand the evolution of the craft. It is

typical that the surviving buildings from the early periods tend to be grand examples, such as ecclesiastical and government buildings: The common vernacular structures undoubtedly didn't survive as well as the cathedrals and palaces.

The majority of the early settlers of what is now the United States came from areas that supported a timber-framing rather than a log-building tradition. In the Northeast, for example, settlers from Great Britain, France, Germany, and Holland all played a role in shaping the building traditions even though each culture had its own preferences for timber species, framing styles, joinery types, and building layout. Some appreciation of the Dutch and English approaches to timber framing can help you understand timber framing as a whole.

The English

The predominant influence of our project house is from the English tradition, which was strong in America, especially along the East Coast and in New England. The first-generation English houses were

▲ *Many wonderful markings can be found underneath flooring or sheathing. These "marriage marks" (see Glossary) were covered by flooring for over two hundred years.*

◀ *This restored Welsh farmhouse dating from 1470, now at the Welsh Folk Museum, is supported by crucks.*

▲ *Interior of Leigh Court cruck barn, Worcestershire, England.*

▲ *Cruck frames may be making a comeback. This one shelters the author's office and workshop in Windsor, Massachusetts.*

Another building system that became popular in the British Isles was the cruck frame. Cruck frames are composed of pairs of large curved or bent timbers that are joined at the top to support a ridgebeam. The curved timbers take the place of both post and rafter, and because they form large triangles, they are quite stable structures. In fact, cruck buildings often lack sill beams as the feet of the cruck blades often sat on large stones called *stylobates*. Historians have always been interested in the cruck tradition as their design seems so ancient. They appear to be the next step up from a lashed pole structure, though this may not be the case as some of the earliest examples are the most refined. An extensive survey has been done of the more than three thousand examples surviving in an attempt to better understand cruck buildings (see Alcock [1981]). Cruck blades were hewn or sawn from large crooked logs. If the log was thick enough, two matched cruck blades could be sawn out of it. Cruck buildings vary in size from humble cottages to great barns. The largest cruck-framed building in the world is the barn at Leigh Court, Worcestershire, England. The interior span between crucks is 33 feet 6 inches and the barn is 140 feet long. It dates from the late thirteenth to early fourteenth century. Though the cruck building tradition is often associated with the English, it can be found elsewhere in Europe.

comparable to homes of the same period in England, though the timbers reflect the quality of the virgin timber found here. In England, the primeval forests were long gone, and the second-growth forests were heavily harvested for buildings, ships, charcoal, and home heating. The English framing system developed in part from the need to use lower quality and often crooked timber. In fact, crooked timbers were used to their best advantage and could even enhance the appearance of the building. The typical frame design was developed to create a structurally stable frame using light members. The roof was trussed (triangulated) at each cross frame, and the special English tying joint was used to tie the roof truss to the wall posts. This joint also came to America and a simpler form is resurrected in our project house frame (see Chapter 3).

When the English settled in America, their homes reflected their traditions with a few variations. The use of curved and crooked timber gave way to straight timber because it was readily available and easier to work. The traditional wall infill system of wattle and daub (woven twigs plastered over with a mixture of clay, lime, and dung) was soon replaced with wood boarding. With the plentiful timber supply and many water-powered sawmills, boards could economically cover a frame as clapboards or become flooring. Riven wood shingles replaced thatch, reducing roof pitches. The forests of America played an important role in shaping the English colonial houses here.

Some builders began using a different framing system for their houses. Instead of framing a multitude of timber studs to support the wall sheathing and interior finish, builders nailed wide verti-

cal planks on the outside of the frame from sill to plate and then nailed horizontal clapboards to the planking. On the inside, they nailed on wood lath and plastered the wall. This system meant considerably less mortise-and-tenon work so the framing was faster and, thus, more economical. By the end of the eighteenth century, New England was covered with these plank-on-frame houses. The project house this book describes is a plank-on-

▲ *This seventeenth-century cottage at Rempstone, Nottinghamshire, England, shows how the builders made use of the available crooked timber.*

▲ *In a plank-on-frame house, wide vertical planking replaces the older system of using timber studs. Clapboards nailed across the outside of the planks and wood lath applied on the interior stiffen the walls.*

▲ *Interior view of the restored four-teenth-century Bredon tithe barn in Hereford and Worcester.*

In **England**, barns were specialized. Separate barns were used for sheltering livestock, crop storage, and threshing. There were also huge aisled barns. Those aisled barns that belonged to the church or monastery were referred to as *tithe barns* and were built to hold the tithes, which were a tenth of the annual crop of farmers paid to the church as a tax. Some of these barns were more than 200 feet long! English barns in America were less specialized. A typical eighteenth- or early nineteenth-century barn had three bays and might measure 30 feet by 40 feet. The center bay had

large wagon doors and often allowed the farmer to drive through. On loose poles laid across the beams above, crops were dried prior to threshing. The threshing itself took place on the tightly fitted plank floor below. In a narrower side bay, usually on the east or south, the farmer kept cows and horses with hay above them in a low loft. Since the hay might reach to the ceiling in winter, hay also kept heat in the animal stalls. A wider bay on the other side of the central threshing floor might be entirely hay mow from floor to roof or contain additional animals. The earliest barns here were timber studded with clapboards, but by the eighteenth century most barns had vertical boards or planks stiffened by horizontal nailers or girts midway in the wall. This three-bay side-entrance barn is the type that historically accompanied our project house.

▶ *A three-bay English-style New England barn frame from the late 1700s.*

frame house. Originally, planks as thick as 3 or 4 inches were used in the colder areas for added insulation. Many experts state that wood is not a great insulator compared to manufactured insulations, but modern insulation doesn't have the thermal storage or mass of thick planks. During the day, the sun and the cooking fire warmed the wall mass. During the night when the fire went out, the wall cooled slowly, keeping the occupants warm longer. Log buildings also work on this principle. In some houses with very thick planks, you can see that a few builders recognized the inherent strength in the planks for vertical loads and deleted the posts entirely, though plates were still required to stiffen the top of the wall.

A few houses for the well-to-do incorporated both timber-stud and plank systems. For these homes, the planks were fastened vertically to the interior of the major horizontal timbers, which created a wall as much as 11 inches thick. Brick placed between the studs stopped drafts and provided more thermal mass.

The Dutch

The Dutch colonists settled mostly in New York and New Jersey in the rich bottomlands. As with the English, the abundance of timber affected the design of their structures. In Holland, barns and living space were often combined under one large roof, but we see little evidence of that practice here in America. The Dutch timber-framed houses here were typically a story and a half, with a wall (called a *kneewall*) that rose about 4 feet above the second floor level to give usable space under the roof. Instead of the bay framing used by the English, the Dutch had crossframes spaced 3 to 5 feet apart comprised of two posts, a cross-

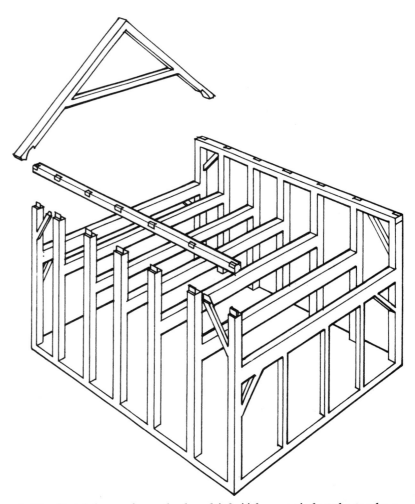

▲ *The Dutch house frame had multiple H-frames tied at the top by a continuous plate.*

beam, and perhaps some diagonal braces. These crossframes or bents were tied longitudinally at the top by plates and at the bottom by sills. Rafter couples with a collar (which joined two rafters horizontally) sat on the plate, with the joint usually over exterior wall posts. It was an early modular system: The building could be lengthened or shortened in 4-foot increments. Floor, wall, and roof sheathing spanned across the posts, crossbeams, and rafters. Usually the space between posts was filled with brick or wattle and daub. Most of these houses also had a lean-to for additional floor space.

◄ Note the through-tenon with three pins and two wedges securing it in this Rotterdam, New York, barn. These tenons could be rounded, rectangular, or polygonal. Long braces rise up to support the purlin plate.

plates. The purlin plates supported the rafters near their midspan and thus carried most of the weight of the roof. The anchorbeam bents were the heart of the Dutch barn. Securing the posts to the anchorbeams was a through-mortise and extended tenon, often with wedges — one of the strongest joints in the builder's vocabulary. The side aisles contained the stalls and stanchions for the animals, usually oxen and/or horses. Above the side aisles were hay mows. As with Dutch houses, vertical framing members in the exterior walls served as nailers for the horizontal clapboards.

In the New World, Dutch barns were aisled barns that were large and squarish, with low sidewalls, a fairly steep roof, and large wagon doors centered in the gable end. The large doors opened into the center aisle and threshing floor, which ranged from 20 to 30 feet wide. Above the threshing floor and supporting the loose poles for drying crops spanned huge crossbeams called anchor-beams (*ankerbalken*) that might measure up to 12 inches by 24 inches in cross section. Together with their posts, these anchor-beams formed H-bents that supported full-length purlin

THE DUTCH BARN FRAME

The Industrial Revolution

In addition to house and frame styles, the craft of timber framing and carpentry in general changed in the nineteenth century. Up to the early nineteenth century, most sawmills were of the water-powered up-and-down variety. Because of the slow speed of these mills, builders still hewed timbers with broadaxes. The mills mostly produced scantlings (smaller timbers), planks, and boards. The faster circular sawmill, introduced in America around 1813 (see Fink [1987]) and usually powered by a steam engine, had all but replaced the older mills by the 1870s, making sawn timbers economical and doing away with all of the subtleties of hewn framing. Jowled posts, tapered rafters, and variations in timber sizes gave way to the standardization of parts. A mid-nineteenth-century barn might have only two timber sizes: 7x7s for sills, posts, plates, and tiebeams, and 4x6s for braces, joists, wall girts, and rafters. Joinery was also standardized. This same barn frame would be unlikely to have any joint but a simple mortise and tenon.

The event that dealt a deathblow to timber-framed houses was the invention of the "balloon frame." George W. Snow developed a system in Chicago in 1832 that used light framing members connected with machine-produced nails (see Sprague [1983]). The advantages of balloon framing were obvious: It used small easy-to-handle pieces of standard dimensions that were connected with a minimum of notching and quickly created a house frame adaptable to any style of architecture. The most important advantage was that it didn't require skilled labor. With a little guidance, most people could build their own houses. The traditional guild-master-apprentice system could be bypassed for all but the largest and fanciest buildings, and the carpenter was effectively replaced by the laborer. Timber framing, however, was still being used for barns well into the twentieth century. Apparently, balloon framing was not trusted for large open buildings such as barns. Today, a variation of balloon framing called *stud* or *platform framing* is the norm for wooden house building.

Why Timber Framing Today?

What are the advantages of timber framing over stud framing? Using 2x4s to frame a house is still faster, requires less skill, and is cheaper in many cases. Short-term economics has always been and still is an important factor in selecting a building system. If a timber-framed home is contracted out to a builder, it is likely to cost a little more than a comparable stud-framed home. But if one compares the life expectancy of a timber frame to a stud frame and considers the long-term economics of the environment and our culture, then a timber frame is far more cost-effective because it is built to last several centuries. We should be thinking in these terms. Economics, however, is not the only consideration. A timber-framed house is stronger and the strength is highly visible on the interior. People feel secure living in a timber frame. There isn't any mystery as to what is holding up the house. The timbers also add interest visually. With a timber-framed interior, moldings and other decorative work are unnecessary. For the owner-builder, there are even more advantages. Building a timber-framed house offers more opportunities to save money by using your own materials and your own labor. It allows you to use fewer manufactured products (with all their shortcomings). You can use your own timber or timber from local forests that was cut at local sawmills, which helps the local economy and saves money, and you can be sure the forests are managed for sustainability. There are also less-tangible advantages: The pride in continuing in an ancient tradition, of doing honest work, and of creating a beautiful house with traditional hand tools.

The Project House for this Book

The old way of building was flexible by design. Builders of the past framed many types of buildings, but they generally only used a single structural form or prototype for each building type, which they simply varied in relative size and in finish details for specific projects. There was no need to design or engineer each building from scratch. Houses were generally based on these classic, comfortable, and efficient prototypes. Often, the great strength of these prototypes was their ability to easily expand and become individualized as the owners' needs evolved. This book's primary aim is to reintroduce such a prototype building system: The hall-and-parlor house.

This house form has been with us since the early settlement of America. In fact, the oldest wood-framed house in the country — the Fairbanks House in Dedham, Massachusetts, which was built around 1637 — is of this form, and the design has stayed with us to the present day. Also referred to as the *two-room plan, lobby-entrance plan,* or an *I-house,* the hall-and-parlor house is longer than it is wide and is one room deep. There are usually three sections or *bays:* a narrow central area containing the entrance, hearth, and stairs, which is flanked by a wider section on either side that usually forms one room each — the hall and parlor. The

THE HALL-AND-PARLOR HOUSE

▲ *This classic hall-and-parlor house, built in 1751 against an older one-and-a-half-story house, stands in Deerfield, Massachusetts.*

"hall" was not the hall as we use that word today but a room where the cooking and eating took place. It had the largest fireplace in the house, usually with an integral bake oven, and most activities took place in this room. The parlor contained the finest furnishings and often the parents' bed. The house may be one or two floors but was usually two. The hall-and-parlor house has been chosen as the prototype house for this book because of the many advantages that it offers:

◆ A couple or a young family will find the design to be an excellent starter house.

◆ The house can be easily expanded as the family grows and changes.

◆ The structure is economical to build and maintain.

◆ Though modest in size, the house is attractive and noble.

◆ Because it is one room deep, rooms can receive natural light on three sides.

◆ The layout allows for a centralized radiant heat source.

◆ The roof design provides unheated storage in the attic.

◆ Little space is wasted on hallways.

◆ The form and structure of the house are deeply rooted in tradition.

The hall-and-parlor house offers advantages in its timber framing as well. Because of its relatively narrow depth (usually 14 to 20 feet and 18 feet in this design), timbers that run across its width can be full length but still remain easily manageable and, in many cases, allow for floor space uninterrupted by posts or walls. With a narrow building, the roof system can remain simple and also avoid interior supports. And because it is a full

two stories, we avoid headroom problems associated with story-and-a-half capes and structural concerns about posts that extend a few feet above the second floor for kneewalls. The straightforward timber framing makes the hall-and-parlor house a good economical first frame for a beginner. It is no wonder that it was so popular in times past.

▲ *Our project house frame makes a good, economical first frame.*

▲ *As in many New England villages, hall-and-parlor houses abound in Portsmouth, New Hampshire.*

Timber-Framed House Design

The importance of good design and planning cannot be overemphasized. Many people spend much of their time at home, so a house should not only shelter the body but relax the mind as well. The house can also provide a link through time if it is passed on to children and can even become a family heirloom. A well-designed home will become a cherished place.

However, there are a lot of factors to be considered in the proper design of a home. This chapter is a primer on timber-framed home design and will help you find your property, develop a master plan, site your house, design your interior layout, and begin to consider the component parts of your house.

The design process itself starts with a *program,* which lists all your household activities and the sizes and types of spaces that those activities require. Historically, most houses have been expanded several times. It is probably better, in fact, that

your plans for your house and land grow as you experience the land rather than trying to anticipate how you will feel about living there in the future. Indeed, few people can even afford to build their dream house complete. Fortunately, the hall-and-parlor house plan is easily added to and if desired you could start by building only a portion of it (see Chapter 7).

Remember that design fundamentally means assessing and prioritizing your needs and wants, so although you may think you don't need to develop a program, you really do. Once you have your program, add time and budget constraints — these projects may have to be phased in over several years.

Finding Your Property

If you do not now own land that you would like to build on, you must find a building site. Where one decides to build can have a profound effect on one's life. A good site can enhance your life. A bad one can ruin it. To find a good site, you must first find a region to your liking. What types of planning and zoning regulations can you expect? Is there a good school system? What sorts of people reside there? Do they care about their land and community? Do your homework here.

When you have found the right region, you can begin looking for a piece of property. Again, you must deal with difficult issues. Is there enough land for a garden, orchards, a woodlot, a pond, or any other plans for the future? You may want a lot of space between your house and your property lines. In rural areas, you should have your own water supply and enough surrounding land to ensure its protection — usually about 4 acres. There should be ample space between your water source and any local sewage disposal systems.

I suggest looking for a partially wooded and partially open parcel. The forest provides a sustainable source of fuel to heat your home, timber for your building projects, and shelter for wildlife. Because the forest shades the earth and holds more moisture than open land, it tempers the climate as well: The forest is cooler in summer and warmer in winter. Evergreens to the north act as a wind buffer, and deciduous trees to the south give summer shade but allow in winter sun. If the entire parcel is wooded, you have an opportunity to sculpt the forest to your best advantage. Avoid clearcutting or too even thinning. Instead, leave clumps of trees and bushes in a random, picturesque arrangement, with large and small trees of diverse species. If you want to attract wildlife, create a gradual transition zone between forest and clearing and be sure to leave species preferred by wildlife: fruit and nut trees, hollow den trees, and berry bushes.

Before doing any substantial clearing on your property, try to experience your land for at least one complete cycle of seasons. Look at how the land drains, where the wildflowers grow, how the sun's position changes throughout the year, which areas teem with wildlife, and even for those trees with the best fall colors. Getting to know your land will ensure that you work with your land's natural attributes rather than destroying them.

Like the forest, on-site water is a good attribute. A pond, stream, or wetlands to the south of the house site enhances views, draws wildlife, and tempers the climate. However, I suggest that you avoid building right on a lakeshore, especially if there are other houses there. Noise travels easily across the water, and other house lights can be seen around the

▲ *When a person chose a building site in the past, he or she probably knew it was a choice that would affect many generations.*

BUILD A CLASSIC TIMBER-FRAMED HOUSE

lake at night. Many feel it is better to have a hint of a view of water (or other scenic features) from the house rather than be on top of the view. A good scene has foreground objects to help frame the view.

Of course, you should also investigate potential problems. Have a reputable company check your water if the property has a well already and talk with neighbors about their water quality. Was the property ever used for hazardous waste disposal? Is there toxic runoff from a farm or industry nearby? Are there any underground or overhead utility lines that may pose a health threat? Are there any long-range plans in the area for large-scale development, such as a new highway or landfill? Would you own the mining or mineral rights to the property? Is there a smelly business in the area? These are just a sampling of the questions you should ask. When you view the property, view the whole town and keep your eyes, ears, and nose open.

Remember to be flexible with your needs. A parcel's size, for instance, can vary in its usefulness by its shape and terrain. The suitability of parcels of different sizes can be affected by factors such as the size of your family, your source of income, and how you heat your home. In general, though, I believe that the more land you can purchase initially the better off you are. If you are fortunate enough to purchase hundreds of acres, you could even consider protecting the land with a conservation easement. If you cannot purchase as large a parcel as you would wish, consider sharing the cost of the larger piece of property with others. You could legally subdivide the land or have a joint ownership arrangement. Either way, you will have neighbors of your own choosing.

▲ *When sculpting out the forest for a view, leave some trees for a foreground.*

The Master Plan

Before you begin siting or designing your house, first consider how the property will be used as a whole. Develop a master plan that indicates:

◆ The house site
◆ Vehicular access to the site
◆ Barns, workshops, and other buildings
◆ Open space for gardening, recreation, orchards, pasture, and views
◆ A woodlot
◆ Your water supply
◆ The septic system
◆ Future ponds
◆ Water- and/or wind-power sites (if desired)

Begin with a property survey drawn to scale. Indicate on the map all prominent features such as streams, rock outcroppings, walls, clearings, and large trees. If your property is not flat, draw in some rough contour lines (you can get help here from a United States Geological

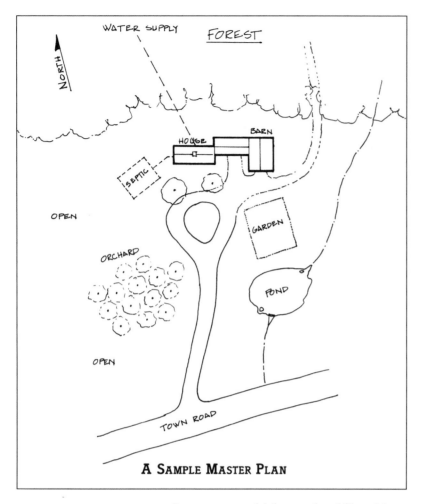

WATER SUPPLY FOREST

NORTH

HOUSE BARN

SEPTIC

OPEN

GARDEN

ORCHARD

POND

OPEN

TOWN ROAD

A Sample Master Plan

Survey map, which you should be able to find at the library). Then add in roads, structures, utilities, gardens, ponds, and other improvements you plan. Try to find the best site arrangement and building orientations. The master plan not only should help you plan how to develop your building site, but how to prioritize your time and resources. Your master plan will undoubtedly evolve through the years as your needs change. It may take a few years — perhaps a lifetime — to build everything.

Siting and Orientation

A common home siting mistake is to place the house on top of the best land on the property. The house would be better off adjacent to that area. If your house sits on the best land, the building process will destroy that place. The authors of *A Pattern Language* (Alexander et al. 1977) even go so far as to recommend building in the worst areas, since by replacing them with new construction you are, in effect, improving the property.

For the house site, flat or gently sloping land is preferred. Such sites ease construction and mean less site maintenance later on. A driveway on flat or gently sloping land means fewer headaches, too. A steep drive will be a problem with erosion and winter driving. If only sloping land is available, avoid north-facing slopes. They often have wonderful views but get a lot less sunlight and that makes the winters longer. South-facing hills are fine. More sunshine falls on a given unit of ground on a south-facing hill than on a flat or north-facing site. If your house is designed with passive solar heating in mind, you will appreciate a southern orientation. Finally, avoid choosing a site that is downhill from a well-traveled road — there will be polluted runoff and annoying vehicle noise. The best house site might have an uninhabited hill or mountain to the north for shelter with potential for a gravity-fed water system.

Designing the House's Interior

Using your program as a guide, sketch bubble diagrams to indicate relative locations of functions and spaces without regard for scale. The diagrams should be simple sketches that experiment with circulation patterns, relationships between spaces, and links between the house or other improvements and the site as a whole. Indicate such factors as how the sun moves across the sky and where the best views are. Do as many bubble diagrams as you need until you have the best rough layout.

Next come preliminary design drawings. Like the bubble diagrams, these drawings can be either of the house or of the whole site. At this stage, the bubbles become rectangular spaces drawn roughly to scale, usually ¼ inch equals 1 foot for floor plans. Graph paper with ¼-inch squares allows for quick sketches to scale. Put doors, windows, stairs, and counters on the house drawings. If the house has two stories, try to think of the second floor as you work on the first. Sectional drawings may also be necessary at this point if the house is not a full two stories. If it is a story-and-a-half design, for instance, the whole second floor will not have full headroom. Because we are designing a timber-framed house, you should also now begin to think in terms of *bays,* which are the spaces between *bents,* which are structural cross sections. Bay widths vary depending on the functions that are designed to occur within them. In the hall-and-parlor house, the center bay needs to accommodate the stairs and chimney. Typical widths for this bay traditionally were 6 to 10 feet. My design uses 8 feet. I chose 14 feet for the bays on either side of the center bay, which is a practical bay size that allows for generous rooms but balances economy. As a bay increases in width, the floor joists, plates, and other beams must increase in size and, therefore, cost. You may ask, Why not for simplicity make the central bay 14 feet wide as well? The design of the house and the design of the frame work very naturally together if the

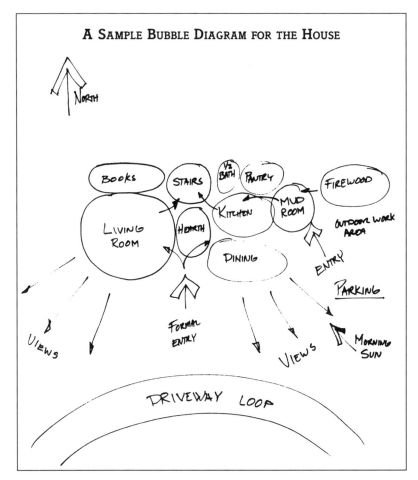

A Sample Bubble Diagram for the House

exposed interior timbers frame the rooms and spaces rather than exist independently of them. If the designs work together, then the timbers enhance and define the spaces.

Design Considerations

I have included my own interior design for the project house. Although this design may meet the needs of many families in whole or in part, other families may find through the design process that a very different layout would be more suitable. My purpose is primarily to give you some general ideas to help you design your home.

In this plan, the first floor is basically one large open room with two primary

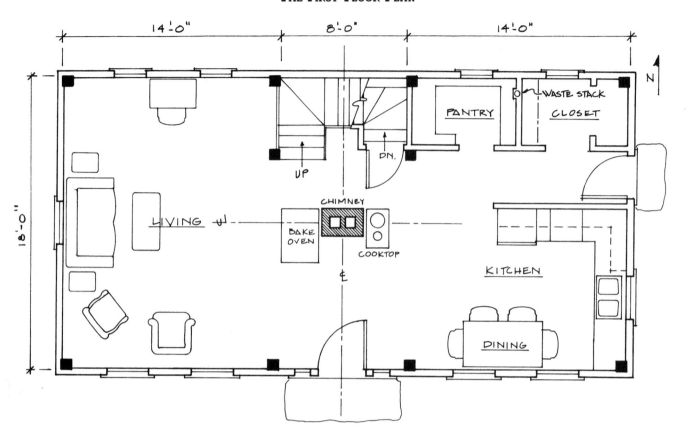

zones: an eating and cooking area and a living room area. A central hearth and stairs divide the zones, which occupy a bay together. If desired, these bays could have interior partitions to further define the spaces, as most early American houses did. With open plans, however, activities in different zones can expand into adjacent spaces, and light, heat, and sound flow more easily (although sound travel is not always an advantage). A single radiant heat source in the central bay such as a masonry heater or wood stove can readily heat the entire floor, but the presence of partitions usually requires a radiant heat source in each room.

A pantry, half-bath, laundry room, and/or closet all work well against the cooler north wall of the kitchen bay. Pan-tries are making a comeback in houses today for the bulk storage of food and large cooking utensils and even as a place for a refrigerator or stand-alone freezer. A pantry as small as 3 feet by 4 feet might be ample. One wall could have narrow shelves for canned or bottled goods. If the shelves are one item deep, everything will be in plain view. Another wall could have wide shelves for bulk goods and appliances. Let shelves extend to the ceiling and around windows. See *A Pattern Language* (Alexander et al. 1977) for more ideas. A small laundry room near the kitchen makes hanging laundry outside more inviting and saves energy. I placed an entrance on the east side that might open on a garage, porch, or woodshed. A small closet near the door is convenient.

Informal kitchen-area entrances often receive more use than formal entryways, especially for bringing food into the house. Also, a clear path from this door to the hearth helps when bringing in firewood. If you plan a root cellar or basement laundry room, the stairs to the basement should be readily accessible from the kitchen.

I did not include a separate dining room. Few families use dining rooms, so in many cases they are a waste of building space. Most people now eat in or near the kitchen. A wall between food preparation and eating areas prevents communication between those preparing or cleaning up after meals and those at the table. In my plan, the dining table is placed against the south wall for ample morning and noontime sun. For extra diners, it can be pulled away from the wall and extended.

Early hall-and-parlor houses typically had an entrance into the center bay. My design uses this entrance as a relatively formal doorway for guests and special occasions, but there is no reason why this entrance cannot be the primary one. Adding a porch and/or entry room could provide a good entrance transition.

The living room zone could be an open 14-foot by 18-foot space. An alcove against the north wall for a day bed, window seat, or reading niche could comfortably set off that space. Otherwise, the stairs and exposed timber framing as well as the masonry heater, fireplace, or wood stove help define this area.

Like the first floor, my design for the second floor is divided into two zones or sections to minimize corridors. A generously sized bath can be placed against the northeast corner to keep its plumbing above the kitchen area for economy. If necessary, you could rearrange the layout and have three small bedrooms. I

THE SECOND-FLOOR PLAN

CLOSET   CLOSET   VENT STACK   BATH   CLOSET   N   DN.   LINEN   BEDROOM 13'-6" x 15'-6"   ACCESS TO ATTIC   ACTIVITY   BEDROOM 12'-6" x 13'-6" suggest placing the bedrooms' closets against the north wall for insulation. In the central bay on the south side, there is space for a walk-in closet, an alcove for sleeping, or an activity room off of both bedrooms.

All bedrooms should receive either southern or eastern light, although eastern light is preferable. By tilting the house's axis a few degrees, the bedroom on the west end will receive more morning light.

Remember to allow space for access to the attic. This access could be a steep ship's-type stair, a larger stair stacked over the main stairs, or a pull-down staircase. The entryway should open near the middle of the attic, because the amount of headroom is greatest there. Most new homes lack attics, which are great for unheated storage. In addition, attics buffer heated spaces from the outside cold. Windows in the gable ends provide natural light and summer ventilation.

There are many other aspects of interior design besides room layout — aspects that most people give little thought to. Several additional design considerations follow that will help you find the best design for your needs and plans.

Geometry and Proportion

Geometry used to be very important in everyday life in ancient times and was essential to the craft guilds. Even though its use was not often directly visible, geometry was traditionally used in almost all structures.

The equilateral triangle, for instance, was widely used in building. All three of its sides are the same length and all three interior angles are 60 degrees; you can draw one using only a straightedge and a compass. But the simple equilateral triangle served as the basis for the Gothic pointed arch and the cross sections of many barns in this country. If you look at the cross section of one of these barns, for instance, you would see that the base of the triangle is the top of the floor and the apex is the peak of the roof.

You may remember from trigonometry that a triangle formed with sides in the ratio of 3, 4, and 5 is a right triangle; that is, one corner is 90 degrees (square). This 3-4-5 principle has been used for millenia to lay out a square corner on buildings and to plumb (to make square) a wall off of a level surface. The 3-4-5 triangle is still used today among builders. It should be no surprise that a majority of old barns in New England have frames that measure 30 feet by 40 feet with a 50-foot diagonal. I even surveyed one 30-foot by 40-foot barn with three bays that had rafters every 3 feet on center in the first bay, every 4 feet on center in the second, and every 5 feet on center in the third. In addition, its cross section was based on an equilateral triangle.

In the hall-and-parlor house, builders also traditionally made use of triangles, but in these its apex was level with the attic floor, unlike barns, in which the apex of the triangle was level with the peak of the roof. It seemed important to these builders that the geometrical form be inscribed within the volume of living space. However, builders more often chose the square over the triangle, beginning with houses in the Federal style built around 1800. If the house was 20 feet wide, it would also measure 20 feet from the base of the first floor to the base of the attic floor, so that a perfect square was inscribed in the cross section of the living volume. The house's length often spanned two squares or, as in this case,

40 feet. Thus, the total volume of living space would be two cubes. For our prototype house, we will use this two-cube geometry. Our house is 18 feet wide and 36 feet long and measures 18 feet from the first floor to the attic floor. Why should we use traditional geometry today? Old conceptions of proportion are still beautiful — they simply make attractive houses. The human eye has always been attracted to geometric forms, even when those forms are not readily discernible. You may be wondering which should come first: geometric proportion or the basic layout. I don't start designing with a geometric form, but I do select one that generally fits a layout I have already created; geometry enhances the home's appearance but does not dictate the design.

The Hearth

Every house needs a central focus, something at the core that defines it. That core has often been the hearth. In medieval European open-hall houses, an open fire burned on the floor of the hall, its smoke rising through the thatch or a smoke hole in the roof. In post-medieval houses, a huge center chimney replaced the open fire, and huge fireplaces and ovens provided the focus for the house. The huge masonry mass was gradually replaced during the eighteenth and nineteenth centuries by more efficient cast-iron stoves, but hearths were still a focal point — a place to cook food, boil water for baths, and dry clothes. The family dog or cat often slept under the stove.

When modern central heating replaced the hearth in this century, homes lost their central focus. Although technology took away some of the drudgery of wood and coal, many of the new types of heating differ in their quality of heat.

Wood stoves heated homes with radiant heat — their warmth radiates through space, as with the sun. Today, most heating systems are convective and merely heat up the air in a room and not the objects or people in that room. The authors of *A Pattern Language* (Alexander et al. 1977) explain the difference:

People are most comfortable when they receive radiant heat at a slightly higher temperature than the temperature of the air around them. The two most primitive examples of this situation are: (1) Outdoors, on a spring day when the air is not too hot but the sun is shining. (2) Around an open fire, on a cool evening. Most people will recognize intuitively that these are two unusually comfortable situations. And in view of the fact that we evolved as organisms in the open air, with plenty of sun, it is not surprising that this condition happens to be so comfortable for us. It is built into our systems, biologically.

Unfortunately, it happens that many of the most widely used heating systems ignore this basic fact.

I propose that we return to the wood-based radiant central hearth system. Although many people now use wood stoves and furnaces, there is a better alternative. Masonry heaters and stoves have been around for a century, are highly efficient, use no fans or motors, burn cleaner than woodstoves that have catalytic converters, are attractive and long lasting, and have the romance of wood heat with little of the drudgery. Only a few Americans have discovered them, although they have long been used in northern Europe. Often weighing several tons, masonry heaters work on the principle of thermal storage. A small but very hot fire burns

▲ *This soapstone masonry heater warms the house and provides a bake oven and cooktop. It can even be the focal point of the living area.*

▶ *Masonry heaters complement timber-framed homes. This 5,000-pound bake oven heats the author's home.*

for a short period such as 2 hours, for example. The hot fire warms the masonry mass, which then reradiates a uniform heat continually throughout the day. Because the hot fire is so efficient, there is little pollution and no problem with creosote buildup. The heaters don't use much wood and can even burn softwoods,

which are common in northern climates and less expensive than hardwoods. The exterior doesn't get as hot as a conventional woodstove, making the heaters more user-friendly and child safe. Integral bake ovens and cooktops can be added, and the heaters can be designed to provide domestic hot water. The only major drawback to masonry heaters is their initial investment cost. But their efficiency, safety, durability, and good looks more than compensate. See Appendix B and Bushway (1992) for more information.

I have placed the hearth between the kitchen and dining area and the living room area since these spaces need the most heat. The chimney also works most efficiently if it emerges at the roof peak. The bedrooms need slightly less heat — many people feel that bedrooms are better for sleeping if they are a little cooler than the rest of the house. Pantries, closets, and other storage areas should be cooler yet, and so the north wall is best for these rooms.

Natural Light

Many studies show that we need natural daylight to keep our spirits up. Morning light wakes us and puts us in a good mood for the day. A home should thus be situated so that as much natural light as possible enters the home, and a home design should integrate natural light in its plans. I laid out the rooms of this design to receive natural light on two sides of every room so that the use of artificial light could be minimized during the day. If the living room area and dining and eating area are spread out along the south wall, they will get the most natural light and solar heat gain.

If you orient the axis of the hall-and-parlor house with its long sides facing

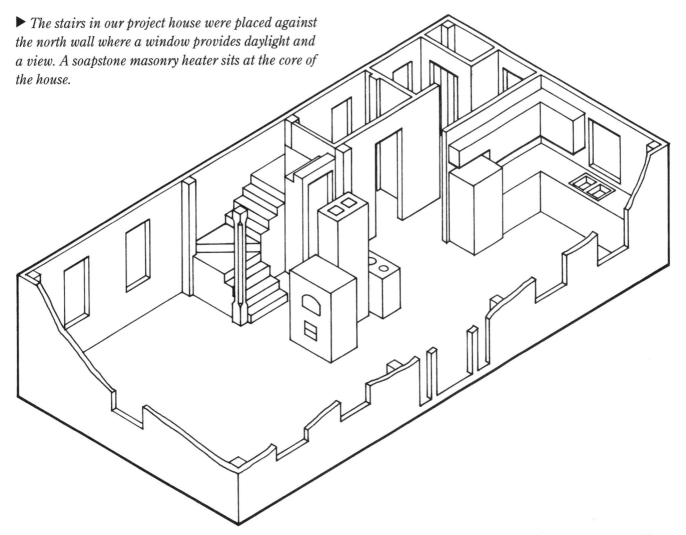

▶ *The stairs in our project house were placed against the north wall where a window provides daylight and a view. A soapstone masonry heater sits at the core of the house.*

roughly north and south, most of the rooms will receive southern sunlight. Sun in the kitchen and dining area is more welcome in the morning than in the warmer late afternoon, so I arranged that area on the eastern side of the house. In addition, because a warm, sunny entrance gives a more inviting impression than a cool, dark one, I placed the exterior doors along the sunnier sides.

There are many simple steps that have been taken in the house design and that you can take in your site layout to maximize natural heating and cooling. You can buffer the house from winter winds with thick evergreen woods to the

▲ *It is important that the dining area receive ample morning sunlight.*

▶ *Use windows with real divided lights for aesthetics and superior natural lighting.*

placed near the center of a wall or section of wall, because in timber-framed buildings a large post and one or two braces sit in each corner. Moving the windows in from the corners at least a few feet avoids conflicts with braces. Light quality is another important consideration. One large window creates a very bright area that makes other areas appear dark. Several evenly spaced medium-sized windows provide the best light in a room.

Muntins also affect interior light quality. Muntins are the wooden bars between panes of glass and are more common on older houses. Besides allowing the use of smaller pieces of glass, muntins reflect light in multiple directions and help to even out the light within the room. The effect is heightened if they are painted white. If their exterior dimensions are the same, a single-pane window has more glass than a window with muntins, but the effective amount of light is greater with muntins. The extra cost of a window with muntins can be offset by the smaller size of window necessary to light the room as much as a window without multiple panes. To take advantage of the benefits of muntins, the window must have true muntins, not the snap-in or surface-applied look-alikes. You need not worry about energy efficiency: Some window manufacturers place a single sheet of glass over the exterior of the sash for greater insulation and to protect the muntins from weathering.

The exterior of the house is made more attractive with muntins because they break up the skull-like appearance of black windows on houses without muntins. At night, muntins also break up the darkness when you look outside and make you feel more cozy.

north and west, and shade it in summer with deciduous trees to the south. Within the house, all living areas are grouped along the southerly walls. The windows on these walls are larger and more numerous than those on the northerly walls. These are all passive solar techniques — they don't require high-tech pumps and fans to make them work. You can, however, go much further with passive solar systems. The house design is flexible enough for this, but such a discussion is beyond the scope of this book (see *The Passive Solar Construction Handbook* [Steven Winter Associates 1983]).

Windows

Windows, of course, regulate how much natural light actually enters a house. How should they be arranged? Traditionally, windows were usually

The Stairs

To keep travel distances and the length of corridors upstairs to a minimum, the stairs need to be near the center of the house. On the first floor I have placed them roughly in the middle of the house and they arrive on the second floor in about the same place. I also suggest placing them against the north wall so as not to waste direct southern sun. The plans show winders — stairs that turn as they rise — as they fit better in the design. Because the configuration of stairs is regulated by the building code, check with your local codes for specifics.

Designing for Health

The architect should also have a knowledge of the study of medicine on account of the question of climates, air, the healthiness and unhealthiness of sites, and the use of different waters. For without these considerations, the healthiness of a dwelling cannot be assured.
— *Marcus Vitruvius Pollio*
100 BC

Despite the draftiness of old houses, their air quality may have been healthier than that of most houses built today. The technological improvements of the modern age came so quickly that no one could determine all of the repercussions. Technology is self-promoting: When a new technology goes wrong, new technology is created to fix it. The building industry rarely considers simply trying an old way — old ways don't create as much business. For example, as supertight, super-insulated houses were developed with almost impermeable vapor barriers, re-searchers discovered that the indoor air quality of these houses was hazardous. A new market suddenly emerged for units that exchanged the air in the house and retained heat from the exhausted air. Now you have to have your air-to-air heat exchanger's fan running 24 hours a day inside your house. If builders went back to a somewhat porous wall system, all that technology would be unnecessary — but that's not good for business!

I would like to eliminate the vapor barriers, but most building codes require them in walls at least. Please check with your local building official to see if you could eliminate a ceiling vapor barrier with adequate natural ventilation in the attic so that air could then slowly move through the ceiling. If the roof above the attic has wood shingles, slates, or some other natural covering over real boards instead of plywood decking, the attic will vent naturally. Otherwise, you may have to provide for ventilation. In either case, wood shingles are the roofing of choice. They don't heat up in the summer sun the way asphalt shingles do and in the winter they insulate against the cold better. You can also produce them yourself — many portable sawmills have attachments for sawing shingles.

Today it seems that you cannot mention timber-frame homes without bringing up stress-skin (also called foam-core) panels. They contain a rigid-foam insulation core sandwiched between two sheets of material, usually gypsum wallboard and oriented strand board (OSB), which is made of wood chips glued together. Measuring 4 feet by 8 feet or larger, the panels are applied over the outside of a timber frame to form the interior finish wall and the outside sheathing simultaneously. They are undoubtedly a fast way to enclose a house and, because of the good insulating properties of the various foams, they make the house extremely energy efficient.

But I feel there are serious drawbacks to their use. One major consideration is that I don't feel that their materials are as permanent as the frame. The so-called structural facings are usually held together with glue and paper, hardly durable materials when we consider the rigors of moisture and temperature a house wall is exposed to over many years. Because the panels are airtight, indoor moisture levels rise and there can be condensation problems in the walls and roof. In my area, carpenter ants and mice often find a home in the foam core. What happens to your home if the panels need replacing? Many of the foams used contain chlorofluorocarbons (CFCs), which are contributing to the destruction of the Earth's protective ozone layer. The glues in pressed wood sheets like chipboard, plywood, and particle board often contain formaldehyde. And lastly, such enclosure systems are squeezing out the owner-builder and local contractor. Because much of the labor needed to construct panels occurs at the factory, most of the money spent on panels leaves the local economy.

Panels have continued to improve since their arrival on the timber-frame market in the 1970s. Manufacturers are changing the chemical makeup of some foams to use lower amounts of CFCs, offering no-CFC foam-types, adding chemicals to deter pests, and using non-formaldehyde-based glues. Some are even using real wood facings. I am taking a wait-and-see attitude.

Because many synthetic materials may cause health problems, I suggest using natural building supplies. Even synthetic materials that may be benign in your house may cause health problems for the person making or installing them. Before you buy a product, consider where it comes from, how it is made, what is in it, and how it comes to you. Remember as well that you may have to pay a substantial amount to dispose of a toxic synthetic material when it deteriorates. That's another vote in favor of using natural materials. Think carefully as well before you buy a new piece of technology. I suggest avoiding high-tech gadgets if a natural system can do the same thing. Good design and planning can take the place of much technology and save you money in the process.

Finally, remember that with locally produced materials or equipment you can know who made the product, where and how they made it, and that a lot of fuel wasn't wasted getting it to you. And the money stays in your locale.

CHAPTER 3

Understanding Timber Framing

Because the craft of timber framing has been with us for centuries, there are a multitude of frame designs available. Culture, climate, timber supply, available tools, and building purpose have all affected frame design in different regions of the world. This chapter concentrates on the frame design of the project house, although many aspects of this frame apply to other styles of frame design as well.

Bents and Bays

Bents and bays are very important to timber-framed buildings. The house has three bays — which are the areas between lines of structural supports — and there are four crossframes or bents that define these bays. Each bent is composed of a pair of two-story posts connected by a girding beam or crossbeam that supports the second floor, which together form an H. Diagonal braces are added to these bents to stiffen them laterally. The interior bents may also have an additional single-story (or prick) post to support second-floor loads. It is also important to note that each bent is numbered, starting from the west, for identification purposes.

The Sills

Sills are the bottom-most part of the wooden house frame. They serve to spread the building's weight over the foundation, to tie the top of the masonry (as opposed to poured concrete) foundation together, to join the frame at its base, and to prevent the surrounding soil from pushing in the basement wall. Most sills

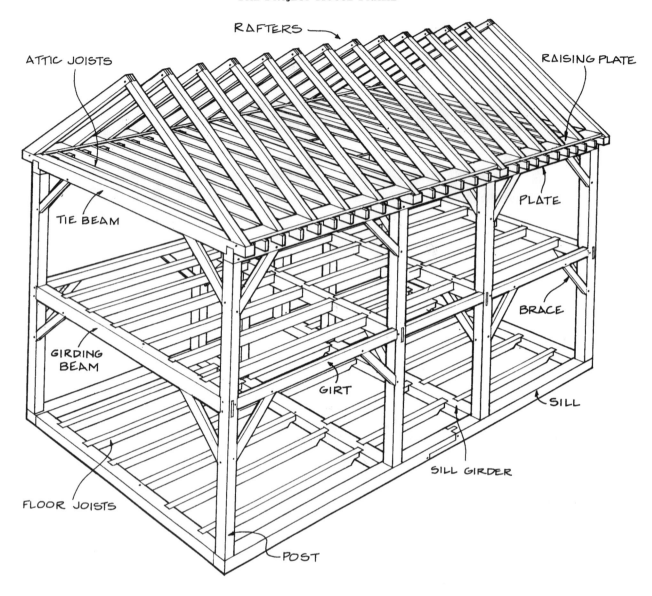

RAFTERS

ATTIC JOISTS

RAISING PLATE

TIE BEAM

PLATE

GIRDING BEAM

BRACE

GIRT

SILL

SILL GIRDER

FLOOR JOISTS

POST

were rectangular rather than square in cross section and were laid with the broad faces flat. These plans call for 8x9 sill beams, a common sill size. All of the first-floor vertical posts are mortised into the sills. Joists may also be notched into the sills and the exterior wall planks are nailed to them. The longitudinal sills in the project house are 36 feet long, and the transverse sills (which span the building's width) are 18 feet long. Although it is

possible to purchase an 8x9 timber that is 36 feet long, you would do better to make each longitudinal sill from two shorter timbers that are scarfed or spliced together. Timbers under 20 feet long are cheaper and easier to procure and handle.

Condensation often makes foundations damp and moisture makes wood rot, so a rot-resistant wood species should be used for sills. Commercially pressure-treated timbers are one solution. Old

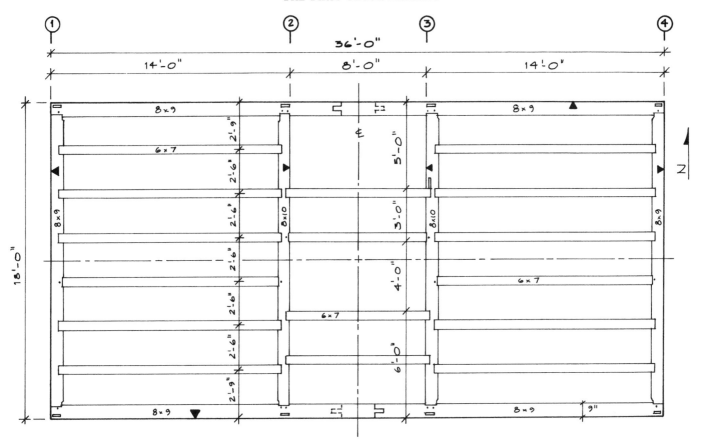

The Floor System

framers used naturally rot-resistant wood species (see Chapter 4). Throughout North America you can find one or more of these rot-resistant species, which often cost less than pressure-treated timbers. In my area of the Northeast, for example, black cherry is a good choice for sills.

The Floor System

Two 8x10 sill girders (also laid flat) cross the basement or crawlspace to support floor joists and any above-basement interior posts and to strengthen the sills at the bents. Basement posts or crawl-space piers support these girders and prevent them from sagging.

Floor joists span the space between the sills and the sill girders. They transfer the loads of the flooring and objects on the flooring to the rest of the frame. On this particular frame, the joists span the 14- and 8-foot bays and notch into the sill girders and end sills. In many old frames, the floor joists for the first floor were logs, usually with the bark removed, that were only hewn flat on the top side to save time and money. Most frames today are sawn, so the drawings show rectangular joists, although log joists could be used as well. At least one joist in each bay should be mortised and tenoned in place to keep the cross sills and girders from bowing sideways as they season. The number and spacing of the floor joists can vary depending on the thickness of

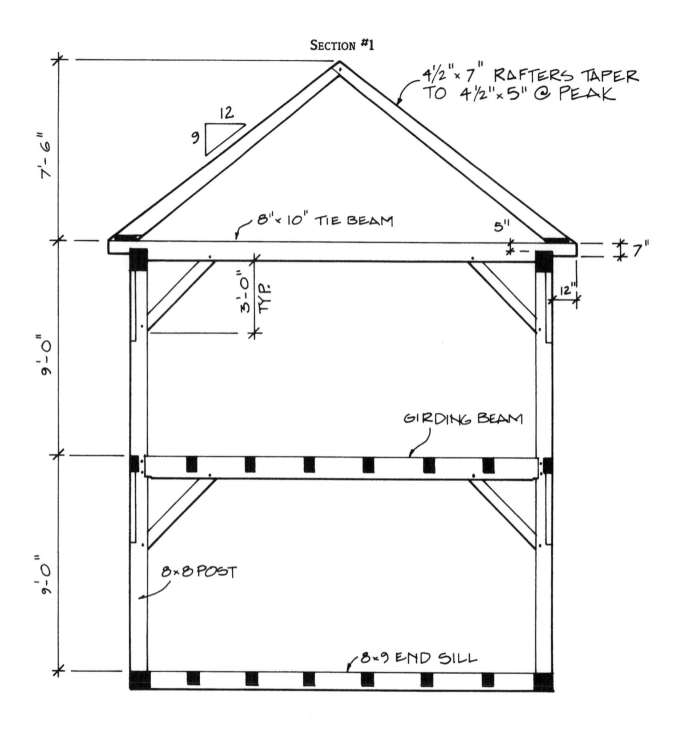

4½" × 7" RAFTERS TAPER TO 4½"×5" @ PEAK

12
9

8"×10" TIE BEAM

5"

7"

3'-0" TYP.

12"

7'-6"

9'-0"

GIRDING BEAM

8×8 POST

9'-0"

8×9 END SILL

▲ *This section shows an end crossframe (numbers 1 and 4).*

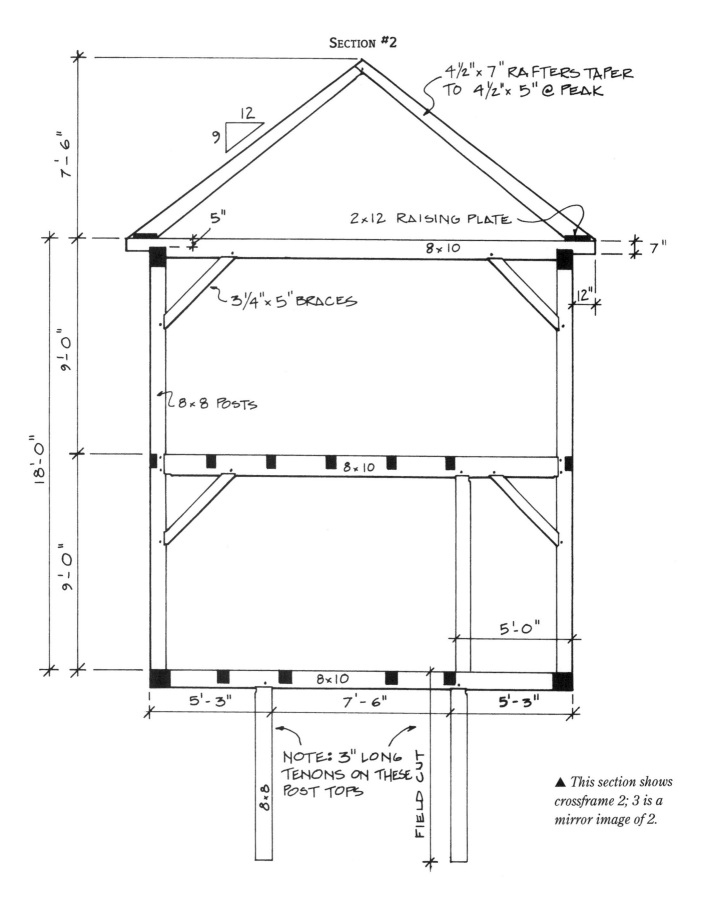

SECTION #2

4½" × 7" RAFTERS TAPER TO 4½" × 5" @ PEAK

12 / 9

5"

2×12 RAISING PLATE

8×10

7"

12"

3¼" × 5" BRACES

8×8 POSTS

8×10

7'-6"

9'-0"

18'-0"

9'-0"

5'-0"

8×10

5'-3"   7'-6"   5'-3"

8×8

FIELD CUT

NOTE: 3" LONG TENONS ON THESE POST TOPS

▲ *This section shows crossframe 2; 3 is a mirror image of 2.*

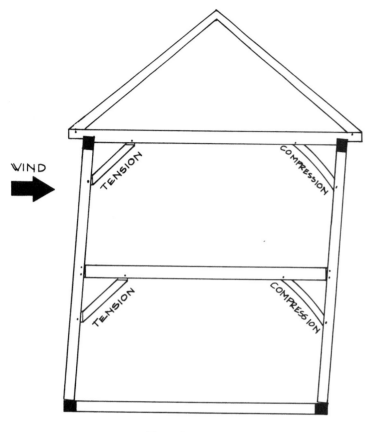

HOW BRACES WORK

Bracing

Open-plan houses that lack the stiffening of interior walls require framed braces. Braces in timber-framed buildings are designed to work best in compression, not tension. In effect, any one brace can only resist force (such as wind) from one direction, so you should always use a pair of opposing braces. They can be placed virtually anywhere in the bent — up to the girding beam, down to the sill or girding beam, or in some combination thereof — as long as they work in opposition.

If you choose to build the hall-and-parlor house as a plank-on-timber frame, braces could be (and historically often were) omitted — exposed timbers and braces were not fashionable in houses after about 1800. Builders boxed in timbers with beaded edge boards. In English-style timber-stud houses (see Chapter 1), however, braces were common and necessary; they were buried in the wall cavity with the studs. But braces were difficult to conceal in plank-on-timber houses. Like plywood in modern houses, planking braced the building from the wind. The interior walls of these houses were also planks, and builders nailed them against the sides of timbers in the floor and ceiling to provide intermediate bracing. Houses without framed braces required temporary braces until the plank sheathing was attached. I recommend using braces where the drawings indicate them.

The Second-Floor Framing

The girding beams are the heart of the second floor — they tie the front and back wall posts together and support the floor

the flooring material and the desired stiffness of the floor, but my recommendations should meet most needs.

Some houses had a more complex floor system with a summer beam that spanned between girding beams. Floor joists then spanned from the outside wall girt to the summer, which was a shorter distance. Although the use of a summer beam meant more joinery work, it might use less board feet of material as the joists could be considerably smaller.

The chimney mass and basement stairs need openings in this floor system. By making the center bay the width of these elements, the framing necessary around these openings is simplified — the headers are simply joists.

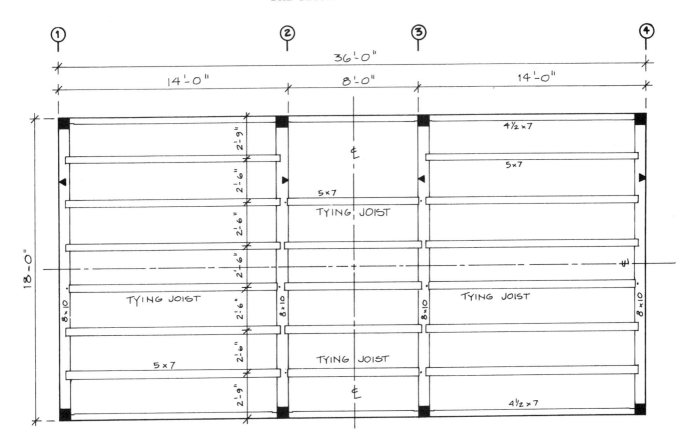

joists. They are often called by other names: *girders, girts, girths, chimney girts, end girts, crossbeams, tie beams,* and simply *beams.* Beams 2 and 3 carry the greatest loads of all the girding beams, so I have shortened their span by adding an additional one-story post.

Horizontal girts run between the posts on the exterior walls. These girts serve as nailers for wall planking and the upstairs flooring and help stiffen the posts at the second-floor level. The second-floor joists span between the girding beams. As with the first floor, openings can be framed without headers and trimmers, and at least one joist in each bay should be mortised and tenoned to keep the gird-

ing beams from bowing sideways. If you wish, you could use conventional floor joists (2x8s or greater) set in notches with plaster or wallboard applied below to create a space to conceal plumbing and wiring. Concealed joists became common after about 1800.

The Plates

The two plates tie the four bents together at the post tops and support both the attic floor and the roof. Plates may be the most important timbers in a frame. Because plates are continuous, they tie the frame longitudinally and, with their braces to the posts, they brace the frame

THE ENGLISH TYING JOINT

The English tying joint was used to join four timbers to connect the walls, crossframes, and roof. Early builders often used a tapered, flared, or gunstock post, referred to by the English as a jowled post, which was hewn or sawn from the flared butt of a tree with the flare placed up. The extra thickness at the top allows for two tenons to secure the plate and tie beam. The heart of the tying system is a lap dovetail joint where the tie beam lies over the plate. The truss or principal rafter then tenons into the top of the tie beam. This tying joint entered the builder's vocabulary in England around 1250 AD (see Hewett [1969]) and was a virtual standard thereafter. Though similar joints may be seen elsewhere in Europe, it seems that only the English examples have the lap dovetail joinery. The tying joint survived in America until the mid-nineteenth century.

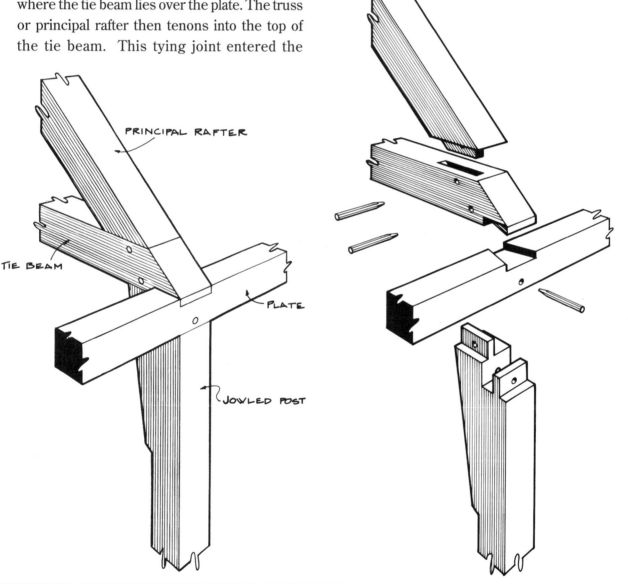

PRINCIPAL RAFTER

TIE BEAM

PLATE

JOWLED POST

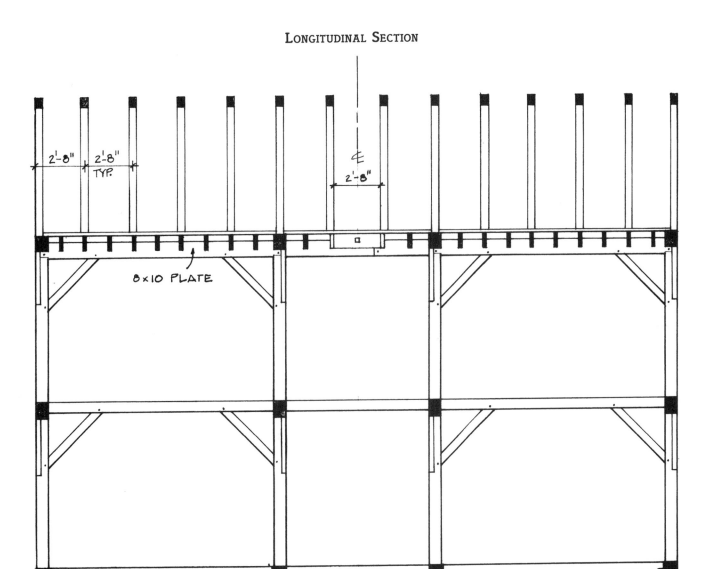

2'-8" 2'-8" TYP.

2'-8"

8×10 PLATE

longitudinally as well. Plates also stiffen the junction of the wall and roof planes. Traditionally, all buildings had plates, even stone-walled structures.

When old-growth forests were common in this country, a plate could be a single timber 60 feet long on large buildings! On this frame, the plates are 36 feet long overall. This is the place to use two 36-foot timbers if you can find them. If not, scarf two pieces as with the long sills for each plate. The scarf should be in the short center bay so that it does not pose a structural problem.

The Attic Floor Framing

Plates stiffen and tie the frame longitudinally; the attic floor framing stiffens and ties the top of the frame across its width (transversely). Over each exterior post in each bent a tie beam with a pair of braces down to the posts maintains the spacing of the plates: This is the tying joint.

ATTIC FLOOR FRAMING

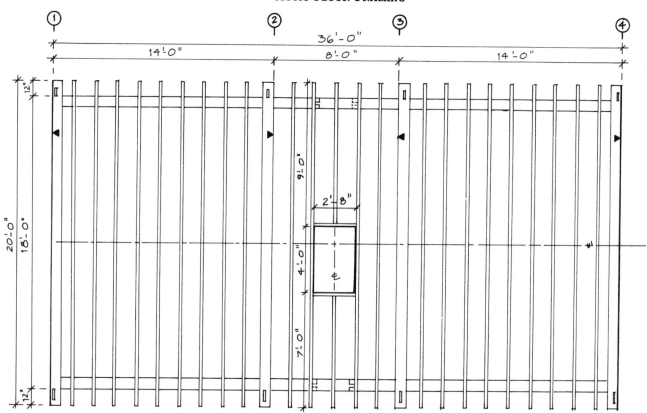

TYING JOINT WITH A STRAIGHT POST

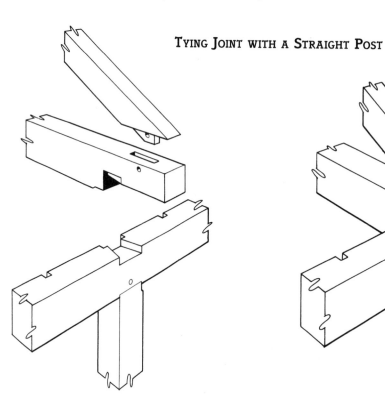
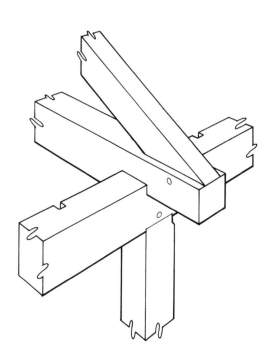

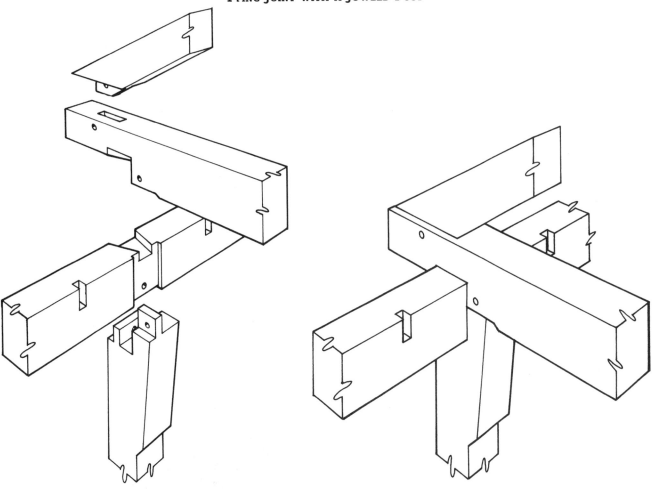

◀ *The attic joists and tie beams extend past the plate 1 foot to provide framing for the cornice.*

▲ *Rafters tenon into tie beams between each bay to create trusses. Between these trusses are the common rafters.*

▲ *A 2x12 raising plate is nailed to the projecting tie beams and joists. Nail rafters to this over every other attic joist.*

Traditionally, the tying joint was the most important joint in a frame. In our frame, the tying joint is not as important as it could be because the attic floor joists are parallel to the tie beams and reinforce them. As in old English frames, the plans show a dovetail where the tie beam laps over the plate. You can also use a jowled or gunstock post to further strengthen the tying joint to resist uplift, which is a good idea if you live in tornado, hurricane, or earthquake country. Note that the tie beams and joists notch over and extend past the plate. The extension strengthens their tying capability and provides a solidly framed cornice and overhang. Cornices of this size were typical of the late colonial, Federal, and Greek Revival periods, and the timber framing was integral to their support. You may have seen on some old houses a substantial cornice on the front but only a small one on the rear, which was a cost-saver. Cornices provide both visual and practical advantages. Even without fancy decorative elements, they dress up a house by creating a border and shadowline between the roof and wall. More importantly, they add to the life of the house by keeping the roof water runoff from draining down the walls and windows.

Although the rest of the frame is 18 feet wide, the overhang makes the attic joists 20 feet long. As with the first and second floors, summer beams between the tie beams are an alternate way to frame the attic floor and thus cut the joists' length in half. Summers involve a bit more joinery work but eliminate a number of 20-footers. If you do use summers, be sure the tie beams receive support from either a central post or a stud wall — otherwise tie beams cannot span the width of the house and support a summer beam at the center.

The attic floor joists are a full 2 inches thick and can be 8, 9, or 10 inches wide. I suggest that the attic floor be insulated with fiberglass batts between the joists so the framing is concealed. The 10-inch depth of the joists was required to meet energy codes, not necessarily structural needs. Historically, joists were often 2x7s or 2x8s. If you use summer beams for the attic floor, shallower joists can be used (check your local insulation requirements) and the tie beams and summers can be partially exposed in the ceiling if you prefer to see more timber.

The Roof Framing

Each tie beam has mortises in its top for a rafter couple (a pair of rafters joined at their peak). Together, the three timbers form a rigid triangle or *truss* that stiffens the roof at bay intervals. On the projecting joist ends and between the truss rafter couples, a wide plank (called the raising or false plate — see Buchanan [1976] for more information) is nailed flat. The raising plate serves as a base for the intermediate rafters and makes it easier to lay the attic flooring — you won't have to notch and fit the boards against the rafters. The intermediate rafters — which have the same dimensions as the truss rafters — are nailed to the raising plate. Most traditional builders placed a rafter directly above every other floor joist, as I have here. Also note that all rafters are mortised and tenoned at the apex and that the rafters taper in depth from butt to peak. Most old frames show the same taper: Small trees were sawn following their natural taper for economy. The roof could use smaller-diameter sawn timbers or logs hewn on the top if desired. If you

▲ *I chose a common rafter system for the roof, which is the simplest, most economical approach to roof framing. The tapered rafters are mortised and tenoned at the peak. There is no ridgebeam.*

choose the latter, the gable end rafters require two flattened sides because the wall planking attaches to them.

The roof pitch varied considerably in old timber frames. I used a 9-in-12 pitch, which is based on the 3-4-5 triangle. This pitch allows for headroom in the attic and was a common and attractive pitch.

The Three-Dimensional Frame

Many timber framers today tend to construct bents that are entire cross sections of the building that include the rafters, much like slices of bread are to a loaf. Short members of one bay's length connect these bents. In the past, however, timber-framed buildings were thought of in three dimensions and in layers. There were still bents, but they were not complete cross sections of the whole building.

Each layer tied the building in a direction opposite to adjoining layers — the girding beams, for instance, link the building across its width, the plates above tie the building lengthwise, and the tie beams above the plates join the building across its width again. The building's strength depended not on the fastening but on the overlapping layers, much like masonry: On a brick or stone building, the mortar doesn't hold the building together. The overlapping or bonding of the courses of stone or brick binds the wall as a unit. A mason wouldn't stack all the bricks directly above one another and then expect the mortar to hold everything. In this frame, most of the pegs could be removed (although I don't recommend it) and the frame would still stand because of the frame layers. The sills, plates, and tie beams are the most important members in this system.

CHAPTER 4

From Tree to Timber

The craft of timber framing begins in the forest. What happens in the forest has a lot to do with what happens in the sawmill, the hewing yard, and in your house. If you spend time walking and working in the forest, your knowledge of the forest will improve your craft. Many framers cannot tell which end of a beam was up in the tree or what species of wood they are working.

Finding Suitable Trees

The first step in finding trees suitable for beams is to pick up a field guide to the trees in your region and spend some time in the woods getting to know the species around you. Try to determine which ones are abundant and which ones grow straight. Learn to identify trees by their bark and shape because much wood harvesting is done in the winter. If possible, find out what the early settlers of your area typically used. Most people assume

▲ *To understand the craft of timber framing completely, you must learn from the forest.*

that oak was the prime species used for timber frames in the past, but even in oak's natural range it wasn't the only species used. In much of northern New England, early framers typically used beech and spruce. Most people cannot identify the species of wood in an old frame: I have heard so-called experts call a spruce frame chestnut. Refer to R. Bruce Hoadley's *Identifying Wood* (1990) to learn how to correctly identify species in frames. In their rough order of abundance, I have seen old frames of white oak, American beech, white pine, red spruce, hemlock, pitch pine, American chestnut, sugar maple, baldcypress, elm, aspen (poplar), basswood, yellow birch, white birch, white ash, and hophornbeam.

The English colonists that settled along the Atlantic coast found white oak in abundance. It was very strong and very

rot resistant and fairly similar to the oak that they had been working in England. The first-generation American house frames were typically white oak. By 1700, framers began using other species in their frames. As settlers pushed inland and found other forest types, they selected the best of what species were available locally.

In their homeland, the Dutch worked with many species, using softwoods imported from the Baltic and Scandinavian countries and with oak imported from Germany. The Dutch used their own oak sparingly — when available — for elements that required durability. Mixed local timber of poorer quality was used for lesser buildings.

In America, the Dutch found both hardwoods and softwoods in abundance. Oak posts might support pine anchorbeams and plates. In eighteenth-century Dutch barns, I've seen huge elm anchorbeams, 40-foot basswood plates, and poplar rafters. Some frames were entirely of pitch pine, a hard southern yellow pine that grew to immense size in the sandy bottomlands along the Hudson and Mohawk rivers. They also commonly used eastern white pine and eastern hemlock.

Base your selection of timber for your house on the following factors:

◆ Local availability and abundance
◆ Ease of working
◆ Durability, stability, and rot resistance (especially for sills)
◆ Cost (some species may be expensive)

I recommend using a mixture of several species. Place highly rot-resistant species where necessary. I suggest using hardwoods for braces and softwoods for the longer members. Remember that you

▶ *The old-growth forests in my area included the sugar maple/beech/yellow birch hardwood forest as well as softwoods like red spruce, hemlock, and white pine. Here is an old yellow birch tree.*

will learn much more about wood if you work several species. My first frame contains twenty different species and my house has fourteen. Over the years I've worked more than fifty species of timbers. You needn't worry about the aesthetics of mixing species. With the exception of extremely dark- or light-colored woods, most unfinished woods look remarkably similar in color. Visitors to my house often comment that the frame is all white pine as they stare at white oak, red oak, beech, black birch, and ash timbers. If you have some colorful species like black walnut or black cherry, arrange the pieces in a logical and artistic fashion.

Each species has unique advantages and drawbacks. The following section describes the more common species in the Northeast that I have experience with. It is by no means inclusive of all the workable species — draw upon local resources if you want to work a wood that isn't listed by asking a local framer and seeing if the older structures in your area used that species. You can also refer to the *Wood Handbook* (USDA 1974) for more specifics on appropriate regional species.

A Short Catalog of Trees

American Basswood, *Tilia americana:* Though not common in old frames, basswood was used occasionally. A Dutch barn in Warnerville, New York, had a pair of 40-foot long basswood plates. The trees grow quite straight with clear, branchless trunks for much of their height. Basswood's soft, even-grained wood works easily but has no decay resistance and little figure.

American Beech, *Fagus grandifolia:* A large, smooth, grey-barked tree common in the northern hardwood forest.

From the study of old timber-framed buildings, beech appears to have been the wood of choice in those areas dominated by the northern hardwood forest. It has dense, even grained, and very strong wood, though it is very workable. Beech hews wonderfully and joints are easily pared across the grain without tearing.

▲ *The author's house frame has fourteen different species of timbers, most of them cut on-site.*

▲ *These old beech timbers exhibit the tell-tale holes of powder-post beetles, though they are still in good condition.*

Because it is fine grained, it can be planed extremely smooth. The sapwood is a creamy color while the heartwood is tan or brownish. It is not rot resistant, so limit its use away from moist locations. It is particularly prone to attack by powder-post beetles and carpenter ants in damp areas. It has a high rate of shrinkage, which will show in your joinery.

Beech has excellent resistance to wear. In fact, the more you rub it, the smoother and more wear resistant it becomes — it was a popular choice for wooden machinery such as gear teeth, shafts, bearings, and items such as sled runners, wooden planes, rolling pins, door hinges, and mallets.

Since the late 1960s, beeches have been hit hard by a fungus that erupts their smooth bark and subsequently kills them. As a result, there is a great deal of beech being harvested at a reasonable price. And though at the time of this writing there are still many fine beeches standing, it might be honorable to use more beech timber in house frames in case the species suffers the decimation that befell the chestnut.

American Elm, *Ulmus americana:* Today, elm has a bad reputation for being difficult to work. Many people even avoid using elm for firewood because it splits so poorly. But old framers occasionally used elm timbers, especially in England. I've seen 12-inch by 20-inch hewn elm anchorbeams in some New York Dutch barns. Apparently, straight, virgin forest specimens were not that hard to work. In addition, its grain patterns are unusual and attractive. Because this tree has been hit hard by Dutch elm disease, it is being cut heavily and logs are available. It would be nice to work some elm before it is all gone.

Balsam Fir, *Abies balsamea:* Balsam fir typically grows along with red spruce in the northern forests though it is not as long lived. It grows very straight with only small branches and little taper. The heart is often rotted on the larger specimens. Its wood is practically indistinguishable from that of red spruce but is less strong. Balsam fir is not decay resistant.

Bigtooth Aspen, *Populus grandidentata:* Often referred to as *popple* or *poplar,* this tree grows very fast and often has straight, clear trunks. The creamy white wood works easily and because it is about equal to eastern white pine in strength, it can be used for the hall-and-parlor house. It has no rot resistance.

Black Birch, *Betula lenta:* Also called sweet birch, black birch is the strongest of the birches and is even stronger than most oaks. I am not sure if framers often built with black birch in the past, but it is serviceable nonetheless. It has a reddish brown heartwood and a distinctive wintergreen aroma when freshly cut. Birches are not rot resistant.

Black Cherry, *Prunus serotina:* Although it was uncommon in old frames, I include black cherry here because of its high resistance to decay. In the northern hardwood forest, it may be the only rot-resistant species available. Most think of cherry as a yard tree, but this native cherry reaches timber size in much of the Northeast. In old-growth forests, black cherry grows to 3 feet in diameter and over 100 feet high. Larger specimens should be reserved for furniture, but smaller, lower-grade timber-size trees abound in many areas. The even grain and aromatic scent are a pleasure to work and its color can accent a light-colored wood frame.

Working stress figures are not available for black cherry at this time, but it is stronger than white pine and you can substitute it in our frame design. I often cut sill timbers from black cherry. In parts of the Northeast, it is inexpensive and common locally.

Black Locust, *Robinia pseudoacacia:* A very strong, hard, and heavy wood that is very resistant to decay. Black locust has a moderately low rate of shrinkage for such a heavy wood. Though logs tend to be more wavy than straight, it is still workable. I recommend black locust for sills and timbers exposed to the weather. Work it when green as it is much harder to work when dry.

Eastern Hemlock, *Tsuga canadensis:* Hemlock was commonly used in the Northeast for both timbers and wall planking. When green, hemlock is heavy but works easily; when dry, it is fairly light but difficult to work. Hemlock's biggest drawback is that it tends to have a lot of shakes. Since hemlock also forms terrible splinters, I often relegate it to areas of the house where hands won't touch it.

Eastern White Pine, *Pinus strobus:* This is the largest-growing conifer in the Northeast. In the past, specimens grew up to 260 feet in height and 10 feet in diameter, though trees of half that size are rare today. There are still pines in Michigan that top 200 feet. It was used extensively for timbers, planks, boards, shingles, clapboards, moldings, cabinets, doors, trim, and ship's masts. White pine is very stable and has one of the lowest shrinkage rates of northeastern trees. It is also moderately rot resistant. Because white pines grow tall and straight, long timbers are easily procured. It has to be one of the easiest-working woods available and where it is abundant, one of the least expensive. Because it branches in

tiers called *whorls,* the timbers will have intervals of knots, usually with clear wood between whorls. The distance between whorls may range from 6 inches to 4 feet, depending on growth conditions. Because knots are concentrated at the whorls, the timber is weakened there and joinery should be located in the clear wood areas if possible. Even branchy white pines are useful if they are sufficiently large as the clear-wood sections between whorls make good shingles. Probably the only drawback to white pine is that if the timber is cut and worked during the growing season, pitch oozing out of the sapwood can be annoying. Considering all factors, this wood has to rate as one of the best timber-framing species. If I was limited to only one wood for all parts of a house (frame, floors, windows, and so on), eastern white pine would be my choice.

Hickories, *Carya* genus: This family contains the strongest and heaviest of commercially available woods in the United States. Though hickories are usable for timbers, boxed-heart timbers are prone to very fast end checking and

▲ *Second-growth white pine timber is readily available in the longer lengths.*

splitting. I have heard stories from loggers about cutting a tree into logs and, while the men ate their lunches, the logs split themselves neatly in half. It might be wise to use halved sections rather than boxed hearts.

Maples, *Acer* genus: Red maples and sugar maples are very common in much of New England, and both are usable for timbers if worked green. The maples have a fairly high rate of shrinkage. In addition, watch out for spiral grain, which is common. They have no rot resistance.

Northern Red Oak, *Quercus rubra:* A strong, heavy timber with a red to pinkish heartwood. Red oak grows faster than white oak and often has trunks clear of branches. It has a moderate rate of shrinkage and works nicely. Unfortunately, red oak is not resistant to decay like white oak. Because of its color and strength, it is one of the most-used species in contemporary timber-framed houses. However, at the current rate of usage, the supply in the Northeast may be exhausted soon.

Quaking Aspen, *Populus tremuloides:* Quaking aspen is similar to bigtooth aspen but less desirable. It usually grows less straight and has more branches. The wood is creamy white with brown- or green-tinted heartwood. Unfortunately, the heartwood is often rotted on the larger trees of usable size. It is not decay resistant.

Red Spruce, *Picea rubens:* This is one of the main timber trees in the forest that stretches across northern New England. Old-growth specimens are occasionally four hundred years old with extremely small growth rings. Red spruce was often used in houses for timbers, planking, flooring, lath, siding, and shingles in those regions where it is common. It is light in weight even when green but is very stiff. Red spruces typically grow straight with numerous but small branches and little taper in the trunk. The wood is slightly harder to work than white pine. The knots, however, are extremely hard and sometimes they shatter when struck with a chisel. On rare occasions, the steel in the chisel shatters! Spruce is not decay resistant and has more than its share of spiral grain. It is especially useful for long, straight timbers and poles.

Sassafras, *Sassafras albidum:* This aromatic wood works well and is very rot resistant. The wood makes fine sill timbers for this design if trees are available in sufficient size.

Tamarack, *Larix laricina:* Also called eastern larch, this deciduous evergreen often grows in wet areas but is modest in size. It is workable and fairly rot resistant. The lower portion was often harvested for ship's knees by excavating to expose the roots. An elbowed section was then cut from the trunk and a major root.

Tuliptree, *Liriodendron tulipifera:* Also known as yellow poplar, this fast growing and often straight and tall tree is very useful. Trunks clear of branches for 60 or 80 feet are not uncommon. Its light, even-grained wood is easy to work and stable. Like white pine, it has a multitude of uses and can be substituted for white pine in this frame.

White Ash, *Fraxinus americana:* This straight-growing hardwood has strong, creamy white wood with occasional brown heartwood. Though straight, knot-free specimens are common, white ash is a little harder to work than it appears. It often develops large checks, but white ash is still a usable timber tree.

White Birch, *Betula papyrifera:* This is a pioneer species and thus is not long lived in the forest. Though it doesn't reach impressive size, it is often big enough for all but the longest timbers. It works nicely with hand tools.

White Oak, *Quercus alba:* White oak was the wood of choice in those areas where it was common. It is heavy, strong, and very resistant to decay. Its shrinkage rate is very high, and it is more difficult to work than red oak or beech. Because of its durability, white oak is the best choice for sills and frames exposed to the weather. Its gradual but pronounced swelling at its butt is useful for jowled posts.

Yellow Birch, *Betula alleghaniensis:* Old framers used yellow birch sporadically in the northern hardwood region. Its golden birch bark is a familiar sight in mature forests. It is very strong but somewhat hard to work. Its wonderful wintergreen aroma makes up for any of its shortcomings.

Timber Selection

Timber is likely to have all sorts of characteristics (usually called defects) that affect the wood's workability, appearance, and/or strength. Most of these are inherent in a living material such as wood. As woodworkers and timber framers, we must learn to work with these characteristics. What follows are a few of the more common traits of wood you need to understand.

Shrinkage

Green timber is saturated with water, and wood inevitably shrinks as it dries. Why not use seasoned wood, which is largely "preshrunk"? The craft of timber framing has evolved to accommodate all of wood's characteristics, including shrinkage. Green timber is much easier to work. Historically, with the exception of certain stock items, timbers were custom hewn or sawn for a job and used green. If traditional joints are used and the peg holes drawpinned, the joints will be reasonably tight after the timbers have shrunk.

However, you still need to understand shrinkage. To predict how wood behaves as it dries, we must first understand the three types of shrinkage in wood: longitudinal, radial, and tangential. Longitudinal shrinkage is quite small and not really a concern. A 20-foot timber might shrink ¼ inch. Timbers with excessive reaction wood or crossgrain are more likely to shrink in length and should be avoided where such shrinkage might cause a problem.

Radial and tangential shrinkage produce distortion and reduction in cross section, and their effects depend on how the timber was sawn from the log. In boxed-heart timbers, tangential shrinkage is responsible for most of the checking. But the combination of radial and tangential shrinkage causes the faces of the

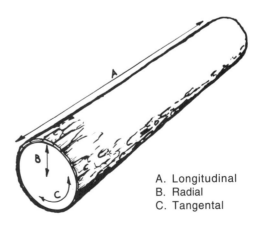

A. Longitudinal
B. Radial
C. Tangental

THE TYPES OF SHRINKAGE

How Shrinkage Affects Timbers

GREEN	DRY

BOXED HEART

HALVED

QUARTERED

QUARTERSAWN

▶ *This end grain from an 8-inch by 10-inch pine timber was cut to the pith to demonstrate how tangential shrinkage can distort boxed-heart timber.*

timber to warp. The face that receives the biggest check is usually the face closest to the heart, but a mortise or row of mortises can also stimulate a check. In boxed-heart timbers, checks are unavoidable. In timbers halved from the log, checking is reduced but the faces still distort. On the halved face, the center might be ¾ inch higher than the edges on a 12-inch wide hardwood member. In quartered timbers, checking is minimal but the square cross section becomes a diamond shape. In quartersawn timbers, both checking and distortion are minimal. Quartersawing is only practical with small timbers or very large logs. This is the preferred sawing method for furniture and flooring stock but hardly practical or necessary for a timber frame.

We must take shrinkage and distortion into account as we fashion the joinery. Traditional techniques such as draw-pinning (also called *drawboring*) joints compensate for them: Offset peg holes put a bend in the peg that acts like a spring to keep the joint tight as it dries.

Another technique balances the relative shrinkage rates of mortises and tenons. Tenons must be cut shorter than their mortises are deep because mortise depth diminishes as the timber dries but the longitudinal grain of the tenon does

BUILD A CLASSIC TIMBER-FRAMED HOUSE

not. On through-tenons, cut the tenons an additional ⅛ or ¼ inch shorter so as not to push out the exterior sheathing as the mortise shrinks in depth. In addition, the inside surfaces of scarf joints and housings must be hollowed out to allow the joint to remain tight as they dry.

Though you cannot prevent shrinkage, there are ways to minimize its worst effects: Use winter-cut timber, so that it will begin to dry slowly before the hot weather comes. Stack timbers out of doors and in the shade. If you are using hardwood timbers and must stack them in the sun, use a commercial end sealer to prevent too rapid drying. Cut your joints in the timber soon after it is sawn out — mortises and peg holes allow the moisture from the inner part of the timber to escape nearly as fast as the surface. The worst checks occur when the outer surface dries while the interior is still saturated.

If the frame is raised in the spring or early summer and covered with a roof, the timbers will continue to dry slowly. Once cold weather begins and the house is artificially heated, however, the frame will begin to dry out rapidly and you may even hear some cracking noises. In fact, you could actually see cracks opening while you watch. In time, the frame reaches a general equilibrium with the atmosphere, although changes in the humidity will cause some expansion and contraction in the wood indefinitely.

Oiling or finishing the timbers will not prevent checking and may actually worsen it. If you do wish to apply an oil finish, allow the frame to season first.

Knots

As long as trees grow with branches, knots are inevitable. On forest-grown

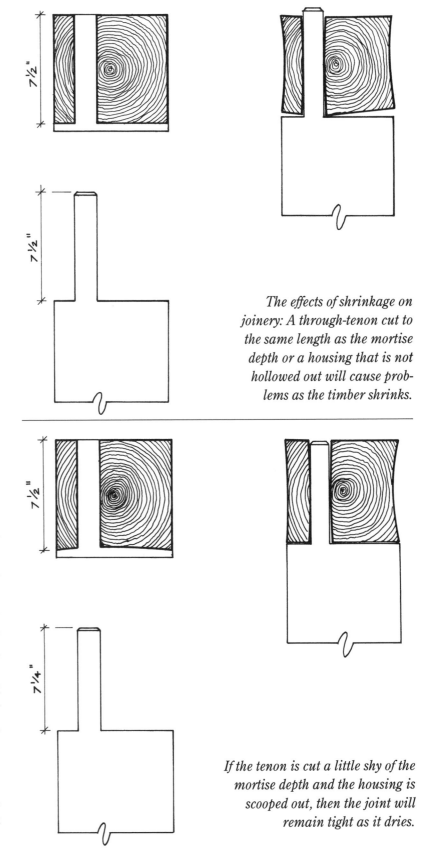

The effects of shrinkage on joinery: A through-tenon cut to the same length as the mortise depth or a housing that is not hollowed out will cause problems as the timber shrinks.

If the tenon is cut a little shy of the mortise depth and the housing is scooped out, then the joint will remain tight as it dries.

trees, the lower branches die and rot off while the tree is still thin. As the trunk thickens, clear wood is added over these branch stubs. Timbers sawn from such trees may have a surface clear of knots and only small knots buried within. When a tree grows in more sunlight, lower branches continue to get light and grow and thicken. Some species such as ash lose branches easily and have clear trunks. Species like spruce may keep their dead branches for the life of the tree. When sawn into boards, dead branches create dead, loose knots that may fall out.

Because the grain changes direction at knots, the timber is weakened and the wood is harder to work. During layout, avoid placing joinery at knot locations. In addition, avoid timbers with knots larger than one-third the width of the timber. On certain species, the knots can also be a dominant visual feature.

Bow

When a leaning or a curved tree is sawn into timbers, the release of stresses during the cutting is likely to produce a bow in the timber. Likewise, when a straight log is cut down the middle, the ends of the two halves typically bow away from each other, and when a log is quartered to produce four timbers, each will have a bow in two directions. If the timbers are oriented correctly, bows are acceptable for spanning members because the loads tend to straighten them. For posts, plates, and other members where straightness is important, however, use boxed-heart timbers sawn from straight, nonleaning trees.

Crossgrain

When a crooked, crotched, or curved log is sawn into a straight beam, at least some of the wood fibers will not be parallel with the beam's edges. Since the fibers are not continuous throughout the timber, it is weakened. Nonparallel fibers are called crossgrain. The checks of a dry crossgrained timber are also not parallel to the beams, and the amount they vary from parallel is referred to as the slope of the grain. Some crossgrain is permitted in graded lumber — a slope of up to 1-in-11 in #1 timbers and 1-in-6 in #2 timbers. You can measure the slope yourself, however. A 1-in-6 slope, for instance, will run 1 inch closer to the edge for every 6 inches of length. Do not use timbers with slopes of more than 1-in-6 for structural applications.

Spiral Grain

Occasionally, trees spiral like a corkscrew as they grow. Some attribute the spiral to the effects of the wind, while others feel the twisting has more to do with the magnetic fields of the earth's crust. Regardless of its cause, spiral grain can definitely affect your timber selection. In *The Craft of Log Building* (1982), Hermann Phleps writes:

There are two kinds of spiral twist, one of which is acceptable for building purposes, while the other may produce major distortions with potential for structural problems. If the twist runs counter to the sun (i.e., right hand), the old-time dictum of the Bavarian carpenter was that this wood would retain its shape when felled. If it runs with the sun, however (i.e., left hand), the bundles of fibres attempt to twist back during drying and in the dried state. This process, which may go on for years, is so powerful that it may force log walls out of plumb and loosen or even force apart roof framing.

Whenever I have seen a contorted, twisted timber in old or new work, the checking will invariably indicate a left-hand spiral relative to the tree's growth as Phleps predicted. Compare the tree's or timber's spiraling grain to a screw thread: A normal screw thread has a right-hand spiral. If you cut your own trees, you can usually spot spiral grain in the bark. Regardless of the spiral direction, however, if the grain spirals more than about 1-in-11, avoid that tree or timber (see the section on crossgrain to determine the slope of the spiral actually present).

Shakes

Shakes are separations between the annular rings and they weaken timber. They are believed to be caused by wind. A single shake in a boxed-heart timber might not be a problem, but many shakes can cause the timber to act like a loose bundle of shingles. Joints cut in shaky wood will cause the timber to literally fall apart. These timbers are to be avoided.

Reaction Wood

When a tree leans, curves, or has heavy branching on one side, reaction wood develops to compensate. In softwoods, this reaction wood often appears darker and is brittle to work. If you are chopping white pine and the wood shatters rather than splits, it probably has reaction wood. In hardwoods, reaction wood has a silken appearance and gives the surface of a sawn piece a fuzzy texture. I once tried to square up the end of an 8x8 basswood timber with a variety of hand saws without success. None of the saws would penetrate more than an inch before the fuzz stopped them. Even the chain saw that cut the log in the woods

◄ *Right-hand spiral grain is evident on this smooth old beech tree.*

▲ *Extreme reaction wood is evident in the end of this crooked pine log. Note the dark growth rings and the off-center pith.*

had a hard time of it. This timber had been cut from a leaning tree.

Because reaction wood shrinks more longitudinally than otherwise, it can cause warpage problems. Avoid abundant reaction wood for spanning members or where it might weaken critical joints. A good use for timbers with reaction wood might be stocky members such as an 8x8 post that is only 8 feet long and carries modest vertical loads.

Wane

I like to refer to wane as nature's chamfer. To minimize waste, sawyers and hewers try to use the smallest log that is practical to get the required timber, which often gives waney edges. In Europe, waney timbers are common in old frames because timber was scarce and could not be wasted. Wide decorative chamfers and molded edges found in more formal framing may have been the best way to disguise the inevitable waney edges. Wane is really a matter of taste. Today, some see wane as an undesirable imperfection. Others prefer wane as the timber still looks a bit like the tree from which it came. I feel that the rounded corners make the timber frame a bit softer and friendlier.

You needn't worry about wane reducing the strength of the timbers — the system of commercial grading of timbers includes allowances for wane. In Select Structural grade (posts and timbers), wane up to ⅛ of any face is permitted. In #1 grade, one-quarter of any face, and in #2 grade, one-third of any face, is allowed. Thus, in a #1 grade 8x8 timber, the wane may reduce a face down to 6 inches.

Remove the bark from the wane and smooth any rough spots with a spokeshave or drawknife. In freshly cut wood, the bark is easily removed and the surface below is silky smooth.

Sapwood and Heartwood

If you look on a freshly cut stump or on the end of a log, you will see in most species a band of lighter colored wood just below the bark. This is the sapwood, the living part of the tree involved with the tree's food storage and production. On open-grown full-crowned trees, most of the wood is sapwood. On forest-grown, narrow-crowned trees, however, the sapwood may only be an inch or so wide. On virgin-growth timber, it is so narrow as to be insignificant. During the growing season, most softwoods ooze sticky sap out of the sapwood band immediately after cutting. Sapwood is also prone to fast staining from fungi and insect attack if cut during the growing season.

Beneath the sapwood lies the heartwood, which is not living. It usually

▲ *Always remove the bark from waney edges as it holds the moisture that attracts insects and fungi.*

BUILD A CLASSIC TIMBER-FRAMED HOUSE

seasons better than sapwood and the extractives in its cells usually make heartwood more durable. In many species, it is also more colorful.

Of all the characteristic differences between heartwood and sapwood, the most important for building purposes must surely be durability. Assume that you cut two boards from the same white pine log so that one was made entirely of heartwood, the other was made entirely of sapwood, and that you installed them both on a house exterior. You would quickly see that they perform quite differently. The heartwood board might last three hundred years and would wear away (about ¼ inch a century) rather than decay. The sapwood board would be attacked by fungi almost immediately and might need replacing in five years. You may be surprised to know that many commercially made wood items such as windows, doors, trim, and even wood shingles are sold with abundant sapwood in them. If more people in the wood industry knew or cared about this important difference between heartwood and sapwood, we would need a lot fewer chemical preservatives.

◄ *The upper log, a red oak, has sapwood that was stained by fungi. The lower log, a white pine, has oozing sap that crystallized.*

Unfortunately, today forests are managed for fast production. Fast-growing healthy trees have a lot of sapwood, and the wood from these fast-growing trees will not last very long! Slower-grown trees might be more economical in the long run if we consider the wood's durability in evaluating the price.

◄ *Traditionally, many farmers became loggers in winter to provide timber for new farm buildings. In many areas this tradition continues.*

Finding Trees and Shaping Timbers

In the past, when a farmer decided to build a barn, he went into his woods in winter, felled the necessary trees, and dragged them out of the woods. He might have taken some logs to the local water-powered sawmill for boards and planks when the spring thaw came, but he would hew the rest of the logs into timbers for the barn frame. The owner played an active role in timber procurement. Today many people in this country are so far removed from natural systems that they don't even seem to understand that wood comes from trees. They certainly don't realize that they can produce timbers from their own trees. In fact, there seems to be a tendency to believe that anything from nature must somehow be processed by industry to make it safe for us to use. The opposite is too often true: Industry often takes natural things that are safe and makes them unhealthy for us.

If you cut and build with your own timber, you and your part of the world will be a little better off. If you have land or access to land with suitable timber, you could use the timber for all parts of the house. Even the wood for floors, doors, trim, siding, and counters can be taken from your own trees if you store and season them properly. Kiln-dried lumber and air-dried lumber only differ by production time and cost. If you plan ahead, your lumber will be properly seasoned when you need it and you will have saved the cost and tremendous amount of energy necessary to dry the lumber quickly in the kiln.

In fact, you could become a combination forester/logger/sawyer, invest in all the necessary equipment for each role, and do everything yourself. Many owner-builders have done that and learned a great deal in the process. If you are naturally inclined toward work in the woods, it may be the route for you. There are good texts out there that cover timber selection and harvesting (see Further Reading). Portable sawmills range from simple, inexpensive models up to more expensive production models (see Appendix B) that allow you to saw timbers, boards, clapboards, and even shingles.

However, if you don't have all that time or don't want to invest in a lot of equipment, you can minimize your investment and still be personally involved in the process. You can select and cut the trees and then hire someone to pull the logs to a central area for hewing or sawing. The selection, felling, and dragging are best done in the winter when the ground is frozen or snow covered to minimize damage to the woods and keep dirt and stones from being embedded in the bark of the logs. You could hire a logger with a rubber-tired skidder or a dozer to drag the logs out but there is likely to be more damage to your forest, and if many trees are scarred in the process, there may not be suitable timber later on. (This may not be a factor if the trees are all cut where the future building site will be.) On the other hand, you could hire a local horse logger or a farmer with draft horses or oxen to do the dragging. Regardless, now that you have the logs felled and located together, you must now decide if you will hew or mill them into timbers.

Sawing and Milling

This phase should quickly follow the logging, preferably before warm weather arrives because logs stacked over the summer will be attacked by sap stain fungi and wood-destroying insects. Logs may be stored underwater in a pond if convenient. In fact, underwater storage can be very beneficial. When logs are stored in water, the sap slowly diffuses out and is replaced by water. When the logs are taken out, they will dry faster and be more resistant to decay and attack from fungi and wood-boring insects.

You have several options for the sawing of your lumber. If you don't consider labor, the least-expensive method is hand ripsawing over a pit or on a trestle. The process goes faster than you might think. With two people in good shape and a proper setup, hand ripsawing could compete with some portable mills. As late as the 1930s, local wood was still sawn by hand in parts of the British Isles (see Linnard [1981–82]). In fact, some parts of the world still ripsaw by hand and the large saws are still manufactured (see Appendix B). The log is secured on the trestle or over a pit. Lines representing the cutting planes are snapped on the surface, although sometimes in the past the log was first hewn square for convenience and then sawn. Some surviving seventeenth-century houses have timbers with two hewn faces and two sawn faces, indicating that a hewn timber was sawn into quarters.

Inevitably, more people will choose a portable sawmill over a hand ripsaw. If you are buying a portable sawmill, consider how much timber you'll be cutting. The least-expensive mills might do just fine for just a few timbers. If you plan to be cutting everything for the house, consider the larger and more automated models. If you plan to do custom milling for hire, get a trailer-mounted mill. Make sure the mill's cutting capacity, volume,

◄Some portable sawmills are small enough to go to the log. For just a few timbers or for timber that is relatively inaccessible, this might be the type of mill for you.

diameter, length, and other vital statistics are appropriate for your needs. Remember that by moving the cant (the log being sawed) on the frame or carriage, you may be able to saw logs a few feet longer than the mill's stated capacity. However, if you will need a lot of longer pieces, get a mill with the longer capacity.

There are a lot of portable sawmills already out there that may be available (with operator) for hire. If the logs are

▼ You can set up a portable sawmill on your land and build your house from your own trees.

stacked and ready for milling, a few days with a good portable sawmill should produce all your lumber. The leftover slabs can be stacked for firewood and the sawdust used for mulch in your garden. And you will still have involved yourself in the production of your house's lumber in addition to contributing to the local economy.

▲ *Hand hewing is a low-tech approach that is, in some circumstances, still viable. With a minimal investment in tools, logs are turned into beautifully textured timbers.*

▶ *A good working height allows you to work without being bent over.*

Hand Hewing

The craft of squaring up a log with an ax has been with us since ancient times. Most pre–Industrial Revolution structures in this country have at least some hewn timbers. In predominantly sawn-timber structures, the longest members were hewn since they were too long for the sawmill. Hewing is hard work but it can be economically feasible if you become adept at it. The first timbers that I squared up were rough and the work was very tiring. As I developed skill and got the right ax, the work became less tiring and more rhythmic and satisfying. With good logs, hewing may be the most economical source of long, square timbers.

Getting Started Hewing. To hew your own timbers, you will need decent logs, the right tools, and plenty of time. The logs should be relatively straight with mostly small knots. Knots consume time and energy. Clear, perfect logs should be saved for other, more-appropriate uses, such as furniture and flooring. Logs with mostly large knots — 3 inches in diameter or more (and 2 inches in diameter or more for spruce) — should be set aside for planks or boards. As stated previously, logs with excessive spiral grain are tricky to hew without tearing the grain. Dry logs are also much harder to hew, so try to hew a log soon after felling it. It isn't necessary to peel the bark, but if you do remove the bark, allow the log surface to dry out before hewing. Because you stand on the log for part of the process, remember that a wet, slippery log can be dangerous.

The hewing area should be on relatively level ground, free of brush, low branches, or saplings that might deflect

BUILD A CLASSIC TIMBER-FRAMED HOUSE

the ax. Hew the log where you felled it if that is more convenient. The chips generated from the process are a potential fuel source and a good compost for the forest.

The logs shouldn't be hewn on the ground. Elevate them on either cross logs or on horses. The ideal log height allows you to hew with a broadax either toward or away from you. The center of the log should be somewhere between 20 and 30 inches off the ground. If the log is too low, your back may be strained. If it is too high, you can only hew away from you. Remember as well that as the chips accumulate on the ground, the relative height of the log to you will diminish, so you may need to adjust the log. My hewing sawhorses are based on medieval illustrations. They allow a log to be rolled up onto them, and notches keep the log from rolling off. Whatever kind of log support you use, set up your work area so that there is a minimum of handling of both logs and timbers. Ideally, the hewing area should be between the log pile and the beam pile. You can then move finished beams off the hewing horses, one end at a time, to the beam pile.

Tools and Equipment. For moving logs you will need a peavy, which is a log rolling tool. Better yet, get two peavies if you have help available. One person can then hold the log while the other person gets a new grip on the log. The spiked point of one peavy can also be driven into the ground or another log and the log rolled in place against it by the other person with a peavy. A 4- or 5-foot long pry bar may also be helpful for moving logs. If you have a helper, you can move a log with a timber carrier, which is basically two peavies joined together. In fact, you can substitute two peavies for a timber carrier. With a timber carrier, you can lift one end of a large log to set it up on sawhorses, or you could drag a smaller log out of the woods. With four people and two timber carriers, logs can be carried clear of the ground.

In addition to being held in the notch, logs need to be fastened to the hewing sawhorses or support logs to prevent

▲*These hewing trestles, based on early illustrations, utilize curved slabs to roll the logs up to a good working height.*

▲ *A timber carrier (top) and peavy.*

shifting. Forged iron dogs were used in the past. An iron dog resembles a giant staple with one end driven into the log and the other into its supports. These can be purchased or you can substitute scraps of wood with spikes.

The process of hewing requires two axes: a felling ax for scoring and a broad-

▲ *The poor imitation of a fawn's foot on left is cut from thin stock and is uncomfortable to use. The handle on the right is well made from thick stock.*

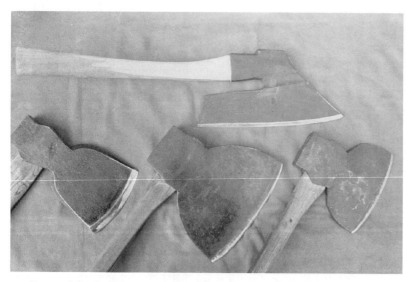

▲ *Some right-hand broadaxes (clockwise from top): Germanic "goosewing" type with 12-inch cutting edge, early nineteenth century; American ax with 7-inch edge; late nineteenth-century ax with 9½-inch edge; and a new "Kent-style" ax from Woodcraft Supply.*

ax for the actual hewing. Felling axes are available at many hardware stores. Yours should have a comfortably long handle and a head weighing at least 3½ pounds. Because this tool will also be used in roughing out joinery, more information is warranted for its selection. First, it is important that the head be properly aligned with the handle. Holding the head, sight down the cutting edge. The plane formed by the cutting edge should lie within the handle. If not, pick up another ax. The handle should also not be greatly reduced where it enters the eye of the head. The handle should gracefully taper to a thin flexible middle and then swell again at the end to a comfortable "fawn's foot." The fawn's foot should be swelled in two directions. It may surprise you that the thinner handles actually last longer than the thick, rigid ones. An overly thick handle will not absorb shocks well and eventually the handle will snap where it enters the eye. A rigid handle also transfers the shock to your hands and shortens your hewing years considerably. If the handle is varnished, use some rough sandpaper to remove the finish. You get less blisters with an unfinished handle. The cutting edge should be curved, not straight. A curved edge sinks deeper into the wood with less shock to your hands. The edge should be sharpened to about a 30-degree angle, though this is easy enough to change. The steel at the cutting edge should be soft enough to sharpen easily with a file. You want the edge to dent rather than chip. The thickness of the blade next to the bevel should be about ¼ inch. If the ax is too thin here, it will stick in the wood and require working it back-and-forth after each stroke. An ax of the proper thickness pops the chips off.

The broadax does the final shaping

with short, controlled swings. If you will be working mostly hardwood logs, choose a broadax with a 6- to 9-inch cutting edge. Cutting edges of 9 to 14 inches are for softwoods. The wider the edge, the more wood you will be pushing through. Because the head's weight helps push the ax, a head with a 6-inch cutting edge should weigh about 5 pounds, with the wider-edge axes weighing considerably more.

Broadaxes are typically sharpened on one side like a chisel, but the nonbeveled side should not be flat. A gentle sweep is better, allowing you to control the depth of your cut. You may find some old broadaxes sharpened on both sides like a felling ax, but they are still perfectly usable. Angle the ax head away from the surface until the edge begins to cut. If the number of surviving old axes is any indication, these "double bevel" broadaxes must have been very popular. They probably served as both a scoring and hewing ax and, as a hewing ax, could be used for right- and left-hand hewing.

The cutting edge itself should not be straight or flat. As with the felling ax, a curved edge makes hewing easier. The middle of the cutting edge should cut at least ½-inch ahead of the ends. The back should also have a curve pronounced enough so that if laid on a flat surface the ax should rock. This curve keeps the corners from digging in to the work and makes the ax a sort of gouge. The smooth, scooped-out surfaces that I used to think were worked with an adz were actually cut with a broadax.

When I first began hewing, I tried those big (12-inch edge) broadaxes with straight, flat edges. Avoid them if you can. The work was very tiring and the results were rough. Fortunately, these axes can be reworked to the above specifications.

Broadax handles are typically much shorter than felling ax handles. The length including the eye should be from 16 to 24 inches. Note that the handle is offset away from the flatter face of the ax to provide clearance for your fingers. If laid on a flat surface, the end of the handle should be at least 3 inches off the surface. Since many old ax heads lack a usable handle, you will probably have to make one. Your handle can be angled where it enters the eye or curved along its length. Use wood with a natural curve rather than steambending a straight piece — I steambent a handle in 1976 that straightened itself out after a few years. Most knot-free hardwoods are fine for broadax handles. Many broadax heads can be hung for either right- or left-hand use. If you are right handed, your right hand is closest to the head and the log is on your left. On some axes, such as "goosewing" types, the eye itself is offset and you don't have a choice.

Once you have a broadax with a handle, you need to sharpen it. To sharpen the broadax, first hone the back to remove any pits near the cutting edge. Remember, the back should be slightly rounded. Hone the back until it is virtually a mirror finish for the first ¼ inch or so. Then the bevel should be filed (the steel may be too hard for filing) or hand stoned to a 25- to 30-degree bevel. With a fine stone, the bevel is next honed at a slightly steeper angle. Broadaxes need to be kept very sharp for good results. Protect the edge during storage with a sheath. A knick takes a lot of time to fix.

You also need a 2-foot long level, a pencil, a chalkline with blue or white chalk, an awl or nails to hold the chalkline, and safety goggles or glasses. You may need a drawknife to peel off any

▶ *When the log is secured, the ends are laid out using a level.*

▲ *Scoring is best done while standing on the log. Make vertical scoring cuts to the line every 4 to 6 inches.*

strips of rough or loose bark where lines are snapped.

Hewing Layout. Space your hewing sawhorses with about two-thirds of the length of the log between them. Thus, on a 12-foot log, about 2 feet will project at each end. Rotate the log in its cradle to its best advantage. Peter Gott, a log-building specialist, recommends putting the crown (see Glossary) down so sighting down the log is easier. Then, drive in the iron dogs with a sledge hammer — not your ax — or nail on some 2x2s with staging nails.

Now you can lay out the log's ends with the proposed timber size. By using a level to draw lines on the ends, the hewn timber will be free of wind. Unless the log is perfectly straight, the timber layout will not be centered in the log's end. You may have to compensate for bows or swells by moving the end layout off-center. Use your judgment to locate the timber roughly in the center of the entire log. This process takes balance, but after some practice you will soon lay out the dimensions with confidence. Don't worry about having some waney edges left. Draw all lines out to the bark

and also draw a vertical centerline, which aids in joinery layout.

The vertical face opposite the dogs will be hewn first. Before snapping your first chalkline, remove any branch stubs, loose bark, or other obstructions that might deflect the line. You can snap a good line on smoother barks, but rough barks require that you peel a narrow strip of bark away from where the line will be. Don't peel any more than necessary or the surface will be too slippery to stand on. Using the ax or a knife, make a slit in the end of the log where the vertical line meets the edge to keep the chalkline from sliding down. Use a nail or awl to hold the end of the line. Stretch it out above the length of the log, lightly snap off the loose chalk, and then lay it on the log in the other slit. Stretch it tight. Now, pull the line directly vertical (plumb) and let it snap. If there are hollows, it may be necessary to repeat the process for just those portions that were missed. You have now described the vertical hewing plane.

Though there are many ways to hew a log, evidence indicates that the standard way to hew in the past was to work on vertical faces. When all criteria is considered, it seems like the best approach.

Scoring. The scoring process uses a felling ax to remove the bulk of the waste wood and prepare the log faces for the broadax. On small logs and areas where the wood to be removed is only a couple of inches thick, make scoring cuts to the chalkline about every 4 to 6 inches. Stand on the log with your feet spread apart and your toes safely behind the chalkline. Steel-toed shoes are a good idea here. Start at the butt (the bottom of the tree) of the log and work up to the tip. The felling ax should enter the log at roughly a 45-degree angle and point towards the butt. An ax of the proper thickness will pop the chips off; a thinner ax will require that you gently pry them off using the handle. At knots or bulges in the log, you have to work from the opposite side to keep the chips splitting away from the line. You will quickly learn the best angles and direction to be the most effective. An advantage to scoring this way is that the chips rarely fly up at you, though I still recommend safety glasses; the hard, brittle wood of knots can shatter.

Except at the ends, you will be guided by only one line because there is no line on the bottom. Use your eye to gauge plumb scoring. You might also check your work occasionally with a plumb bob or level to keep it roughly vertical. The depth of scoring is important. If you score too deep, the finished piece will be missing some wood. If not deep enough, the broadax work will be tedious. Perfect scoring makes the broadax work easy and leaves evenly spaced shallow cuts in the finished timber.

Juggling. When more than a couple of inches of wood must be removed, use a time- and effort-saving approach called juggling. Cut a V-notch with the felling ax to the chalkline at intervals of 1 to 2 feet. Locate these notches at the knots if practical. Then split these sections off, starting at the tip end and working down the log. With the large sections removed, rescore the surface every 4 to 6 inches as above.

Juggling works best on the straighter logs. On wavy logs take care to prevent splits from running into your line. Because of their natural taper, most logs only need juggling near the butt end.

▲ *On larger logs, juggling will remove the bulk of the wood quickly. Notches are cut to the line and the chunks in between are split off.*

▲ *With practice, you can work to the line with a minimum of strokes.*

▲ *After splitting off the juggles, rescore the remaining wood to the line. Now the log is ready for the broadax.*

Hewing. Now that the log's fibers are scored roughly to the finished plane, you are ready for the broadax. You scored up the log, now you hew down the log. Starting at the tip, slice away the wood to create a plumb face that splits the chalkline. If you are right handed, the log is to your left. If you are left handed, the log is to your right. Depending on which way the log is lying and whether you are right- or left-handed, you may face the butt or the tip. I prefer to hew backing up (facing the tip). Unless the logs are all stacked with butts at the same end, you may have to work both ways.

Using the broadax requires some practice, but it rarely needs hard swinging. Since it is heavy, let its weight push it through the wood. Your right hand (if you are right handed) should be closest to the head and does most of the work. Use short, controlled strokes. Without control, you risk slicing into your leg. Again, steel-toed shoes are a good idea. The broadax should be angled toward you if you are working backward, and angled away from you if you are working forward.

The combination of the swing and the angle on the ax creates a slicing action that removes wood easily with little tearing of grain. At knots and changes in grain direction, change the angle of approach to minimize tearing.

Again, try to split the chalkline as you hew. Check the verticality of the face occasionally with a level or plumb bob. If you follow the line and keep your face plumb, the surface will be amazingly flat.

When finished with the first face, loosen the dogs and turn that face up. Rotate the log until the centerline is exactly level and refasten the log. Then snap a chalkline for the second face. Remember to pull the line up plumb to snap it. Since this line is on a flattened face, it should be clear and easy to follow. Repeat the scoring and hewing process until the log is completely squared.

Depending on your setup, you may be able to score and hew both vertical faces before turning the log. You will have to move the dogs, however. On long logs, the log may bow if you remove wood from only one side. If you then snap straight lines on a slightly bowed log, you can end up with a timber that is somewhat thicker in the middle than at the ends. If you are hewing long logs (over 16 feet), snap a line for each vertical face and hew both before rotating.

Hewing Variations. Some prefer to stand on the ground while scoring and work the top surface. Some turn the surface to be hewed at roughly a 45-degree angle. In these cases, two chalklines are necessary. I have found that I receive a lot of chips in the face with these methods, so wear eye or face protection if you try them. Unfortunately, the lines should be snapped in the vertical position before

JOEL LIBRIZZI, THE BERKSHIRE EAGLE

▶ *Starting at the tip end, hew the face plumb and to the line. Position your sighting eye directly above the line.*

BUILD A CLASSIC TIMBER-FRAMED HOUSE

◄ This 10-inch by 13-inch white pine timber measures 32 feet long and took 14 hours to hew.

the log is turned and scored. Afterward, you must again turn it back vertically for the broadax. This is extra handling. The advantages to these variations are that when you are scoring, you are standing straight rather than bending over, and that your feet are in a less dangerous position. Some hewers like to use a long, straight-handled broadax and stand on the log to hew the vertical face. This method seems to have less control.

Regardless of your hewing method, scoring with a chain saw can be a shortcut if the logs are oversized. But you should stay at least an inch or so away from the line. Juggle the big chunks off and rescore with the ax. Remember, it is the scoring marks from the ax — not the marks of a chain saw — that give a timber its distinctive hewn look.

Adzing. I used to think that the smoother hewn timbers were finished with the adz. In fact, I've adzed quite a few timbers in the past. But if one examines old hewn timbers carefully, the evidence shows that the smooth, scooped cuts were done with a broadax. The tool marks show that

a cutting edge was used in a slicing motion, which is nearly an impossible feat with an adz. I believe the adz was used in house construction for tasks such as leveling high spots in floor joists, shaping joist and rafter ends to fit their notches, adjusting the thickness of flooring when it ran over joists, and scarfing clapboards when they lapped, and I believe that the adz still has a place for all of those tasks. But I do not believe that adzes were often used to smooth timbers.

◄ Even odd pieces such as this five-sided ridgebeam can be hewn easily. Keep the face to be hewn vertical when that side is finished, then rotate the log to the next side.

Finding a Sawyer

If you choose to use commercially milled wood, you should find a good sawyer. Here in the Northeast there are many small family-run sawmills tucked away in the forested hills. Chances are good that one of them has the right logs for a project, although your part of the country may not have many mills. The smaller and less mechanized the mill, the more reasonably priced the timbers will be. Speed isn't really a factor anyway. The larger mills aren't necessarily faster, and if you can get just a few timbers to start with, the mill can have some time to cut up the rest. If you get all your timbers delivered first and then spend six months working them up, some will be dry and difficult to work toward the end. Getting small batches delivered periodically is a good arrangement.

Before you pick a sawyer, check out his or her work. Are the timbers fairly square, consistent in size, stacked properly to prevent staining, and free of scarring or grease stains from handling? Rough saw cuts indicate dull blades or improperly set teeth. A good sawyer takes the time to keep the mill in top running condition. Don't be fooled by the

TIMBER	QUANTITY	SIZE	LENGTH	GRADE	BD. FT.
FIRST-FLOOR FRAMING					
Posts, basement	4	8x8	8	#2	171
Sill girders	2	8x10	18	#1	240
Sills, end	2	8x9	18	#2	216
Sills, long	4	8x9	20	#2	480
Joists	12	6x7	14	#1	588
Joists	4	6x7	10	#1	140
MAIN FRAME					
*Posts (main)	8	8x8	18	#1	768
Posts (prick)	2	8x8	10	#2	107
Girding beams	4	8x10	18	#1	480
Girts	4	4½x7	14	#1	147
Girts	2	4½x7	10	#1	53
Joists	12	5x7	14	#1	490
Joists	5	5x7	10	#1	146
Plates	4	8x10	20	#1	534
Tie beams	4	8x10	20	#1	534
*Braces	16	3¼x5	10	#2	217
Attic joists	22	2x10	20	#1	734
Attic joists	3	2x10	10	#1	50
Raising plates	4	2x12	14	#2	112
Raising plates	2	2x12	10	#2	40
Rafters	28	4½x7 to 4½x5	14	#1	882
TOTAL BOARD FOOTAGE					7,129

*These timbers must be a hardwood species.

◄ *Small local saw-mills can offer quality timber at a reasonable price. Don't be fooled by the rough structures that usually house them — a finely tuned machine may lie within.*

rough structures that usually house sawmills — a finely tuned machine may lie within.

Ordering. The two-story (18 foot) posts and the braces should be a hardwood species. In the Northeast, oak, maple, beech, birch, hickory, ash, black cherry, and locust are all suitable. All other timbers can be eastern white pine or a stronger species. See the *Wood Handbook* (USDA 1974) for a comparison of strengths. To the left is the list of timbers you will need for the project house.

The list includes exactly the number of pieces required. However, you probably need to order additional pieces in case of mistakes or defective timbers.

When you give the sawyer the lumber list, take some time to describe what kind of timber you expect. If you give a range of species to choose from, the sawyer's work will be easier and faster. Otherwise, the mill might have to wait until a logger brings in enough of the par-

ticular species that you desire. Tell the sawyer how much wane you'll accept, what size knots are permitted, and how much spiral grain or crossgrain you will accept. Talk about preventing sap stain, how the timbers are handled and delivered, and anything else that might affect the appearance.

The common delivery unloading method seems to be dumping. Unloading by hand does the least damage but requires much more labor. Have it dumped next to your stacking area so that you can move logs one end at a time to your timber pile.

Stacking Timber

The timber should be stacked the same or next day if possible. Elevate the base for each pile at least a foot or so off the ground to provide for air movement below and allow a lawnmower underneath to keep vegetation from growing up through the pile. Provide cross supports every 6 or 8 feet on center to prevent the

▶ *Using short 2x4s, seventeen people carried this 40-foot long barn timber easily.*

timbers from sagging. Sight down the supports to make sure they all lie in the same plane. A pile that slopes lengthwise a few inches is good, so that if rain gets in, it will run off.

All pieces in a layer should be spaced at least 1 inch apart with at least 2 inches between layers. The stickers (spacers be-

▶▲ *This timber transport was made from two trailer wheels and allows one person to move large timbers on fairly level ground. Place each timber so that its midpoint or balance point is centered on the transport.*

tween layers) should be 2x2s or larger, of dry stock, and positioned above the supports. The brace stock can be used for stickers if necessary. Only cover the top of the pile, using old sheet metal roofing, lapped plywood sheets, or tarps to keep out the rain and sun but still allow free air movement. A shady location for storage and working is recommended.

The ideal working area is parallel with and lying between the rough and finished piles. This means that one person can move a timber one end at a time from the stockpile to the sawhorses and then to the finished stack.

If timbers have to be moved, there are a number of ways to do it without hurting yourself. Avail yourself of others that can help. With many people helping, you can use 4-foot long 2x4s, pipes, or bars that can be slipped under the timber. Then pairs of people can lift and carry the timber comfortably. Timbers can also be rolled on 3- or 4-inch PVC pipe or wooden rollers. A plank roadway can be set up on sawhorses to roll them on. A more mobile solution is to make a two-wheeled timber carrier with rubber tires. If a timber needs to be elevated, use a lever or inclined plane. These simple machines have been with us for thousands of years, but you might not think of using them. You don't need to strain yourself.

───────────── CHAPTER 5 ─────────────

Laying Out and Cutting Timbers

Layout Systems

There were two traditional timber-frame layout systems in use here in America in the past. The older system brought here from Europe was the *Scribe Rule*. Framers set out timbers in a yard or on a framing floor in the proposed configuration and then custom-mated (or *scribed*) each of the joints. After a bent was framed, the pieces were marked for future identification and disassembled. The process involved handling each timber a lot as sections were repeatedly assembled and taken apart, but it did facilitate the use of the crooked and waney timber typical of Europe.

Around 1800, a newer system, possibly developed here in America, began to replace the Scribe Rule. Called the *Square Rule,* this system did not require preassembly. Pieces were prefabricated individually to set dimensions, and timbers such as rafters, braces, and joists

became interchangeable. There was much less handling of timber. Edward Shaw wrote in the 1830s about the Square Rule:

This principle is considered more simple than the Scribe Rule, as it can be applied in many cases with less help and more convenience.

▲ *Crooked, waney timber poses no problems with the Scribe Rule.*

In order to make a good frame of any considerable magnitude, it should be the first care of the master workman (after examining the plan of the frame with care), to make out a proper schedule of the various sizes of the timber. Set down their appropriate marks on the schedule. It is of importance that all mortices, tenons, pin-holes, & c. should be struck with a patron [could mean a *pattern*, which probably refers to the framing square]*; for striking, it should be governed by the appropriate lines. This method has the preference in detached framing: the timber admitting of being framed in different places, and not tried together until its raising.*

The Square Rule is based on the idea that within every rough timber lies a slightly smaller perfect timber that is straight, square, and consistent in size. All joints are cut to this perfect inner timber. For example, the sawyer calls a timber an 8x8, but the timber may actually measure 7¾ inches by 8⅛ inches. With the Square Rule, you might frame the timber as if it were a perfect 7 inches by 7 inches. It is unnecessary for whole timbers to be exactly sized with this system — only the joints. Rough-hewn or sawn timbers can be framed to make a square, plumb, and level frame. Even the bracing will fit perfectly. Before you begin laying out timbers, you must first determine what dimensions timbers will be framed to, which is related to the maximum variation in your timber. Timbers cut oversize are not a concern. If timbers vary less than ½ inch from what you require, frame them down to the next smaller ½-inch size. Thus, an 8x8 will be framed to 7½ inches by 7½ inches. If the variation is even greater, frame the timbers a whole

inch smaller to 7 inches by 7 inches. If an 8-inch timber comes out of the sawmill less than 7 inches, you would be wise to get another sawyer. Remember that all components need not be framed down the same amount, but all timbers of one type should be. For the house from which many of the photos in this chapter are taken, we framed most timbers to the ½-inch smaller size while braces were framed to the next smaller ¼-inch size, and the measured drawings all reflect these adjustments.

Tools for Layout

The chief tool in timber-frame layout is the framing square. You can use framing squares for more than squaring up your work. Among many other possibilities, they can lay out angle cuts and act as a template to lay out peg holes and joinery. Some squares have tables stamped into them that help you determine board footage, rafter lengths, and even brace lengths. The square that we use today has remained virtually unchanged since the advent of the Square Rule two hundred years ago. It is not a coincidence that the body (or *blade*) of the square is 2 inches wide and that for softwood frames, a 2-inch tenon, 2 inches from the edge is common, or that the shorter part (or *tongue*) is 1½ inches wide and that for hardwoods, a 1½-inch tenon 1½ inches from the edge is typical. Thus, framing squares are also templates for laying these tenons out.

When buying a square, look for one that is square (obviously). Numbers should be stamped in rather than painted on. Avoid those with tenths or twelfths graduations. The widths of the blade and tongue should be slightly less than 2 inches and 1½ inches respectively for a pencil or scribe allowance. I prefer steel

BUILD A CLASSIC TIMBER-FRAMED HOUSE

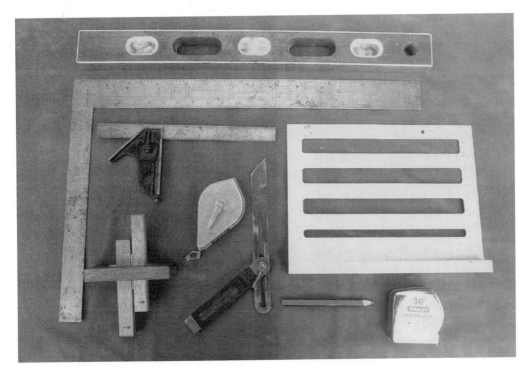

◄*Shown are layout tools: a level, a framing square, a combination square, a marking gauge, a chalkline, a sliding bevel, a Borneman layout guide (see Appendix B), a pencil, and a retractable tape measure.*

squares as aluminum versions are easily worn if you use a scribe or knife against them.

A combination square is very useful for both laying out and checking joints and with a pencil can be used as a marking gauge. A combination square is not useful for squaring timbers, however, since it's not long enough to get an accurate reading of squareness on a rough-sawn timber.

In the past, measuring was done with a pair of dividers that were walked out along a line. The dividers were set to a specific length with a 2-foot rule. For repetitive measurements, wooden sticks marked with common lengths would be used. Today, timber framers mostly use retractable tape measures. For this project, you will need a 20-foot long or longer tape.

Layout lines can be made with pencil, ink, or the traditional dividers. Pencil and ink show up well during cutting but, unfortunately, in the finished work as well. The marks scratched in by the dividers are less visible and can be left in the finished work. The scratch marks also score the wood prior to boring and cutting and thus save a step. You can also use a marking knife, but these marks show up less well. I often use a medium or hard pencil and draw light lines.

A marking gauge can be used on sawn timbers to lay out joinery. One with two knives can scribe both sides of a mortise or tenon at the same time. Be sure to get one with at least a 4-inch long fence; the small ones designed for planed wood will not work satisfactorily with rough-sawn timber edges.

A Guide to Timber Layout

This section looks at how to use the Square Rule, assuming that you are working with rough-sawn members. Square Rule layout on hewn work is the same in theory but is applied somewhat differently

LAYING OUT AND CUTTING TIMBERS

and will be addressed later. Whether you are using rough-sawn or hewn members, however, remember that you must repeat this procedure for each piece.

Begin by checking the dimensions of the piece against the lumber list to be sure it is the right size and length for the member you wish to cut. Set it on the sawhorses. Locate that member on the drawing to see how it is used.

Inspect the piece for defects that might compromise it structurally or visually. Does it have excessive crossgrain, a huge knot cluster, bad shake, or other defects? Is it unattractive? How many faces will be visible in the finished house? If necessary, set it aside.

Sight down each of the four edges to determine if they are straight or bowed. If it is to be a spanning member such as a sill, sill girder, floor joist, tie beam, girding beam, girt, or rafter, rotate the timber until the bow (also called a crown in this case) is up. The face that is up should be the right width face — the 8-inch face of the girding beam should be up, for example. This face is our *best face*. The best face will typically receive flooring, wall sheathing, and roof sheathing; joinery will be flush with and laid out from this face; peg holes will be laid out, bored, and driven from this face; and identification marks will be cut into this face. If you are laying out a brace, post, or plate, put the straightest face up, since it is our *best face* for these members. Strangely, you may find that in some pieces with a bowed face, the opposite face is straight because timbers bow as each face is sawed.

Next, determine which of the two adjacent faces can serve as a secondary reference face. This secondary face, called the *best edge,* should be the face that is the closest to being square (use the framing square to check) with the best face and also the straightest. Some joints and peg holes will be laid out from this face, too.

Put an arrow on the best face that points towards the best edge. On the individual joint drawings, the best face is indicated by a blackened arrow that points to the best edge. When the drawings don't show the best face, a nonblackened arrow on the best edge points towards the adjacent best face.

Check the best face for twist. Put the blade of a square across each end of the face with the tongues hanging down and sight across the squares. If they are not in the same plane, the timber is said to be *out of wind.* If they are out of wind or if you don't have a straight or square edge on the timber, either get a new piece or see the section on laying out hand-hewn timbers.

Lay your measuring tape out on the timber and lock it to the proper length. For tenoned members, set it to the shoulder-to-shoulder length of the members, which is the length without tenons. With the Square Rule, this length is simple to figure. Let's look at an end sill as an example. The building is 18 feet wide exactly. The end sill tenons into a 9-inch sill at each end. Since these 9-inch sills are framed to the next smaller ½-inch size, or 8½ inches, deduct this amount from each end. Thus, our shoulder-to-shoulder length is 18 feet minus 17 inches or 16 feet 7 inches exactly. When we lay out work, this shoulder-to-shoulder length is the one to work with — the overall length is less important. Now, move the tape measure up and down the timber to position the piece to its best advantage, but allow enough extra at the ends for the tenons. Avoid knots and defects at join-

BUILD A CLASSIC TIMBER-FRAMED HOUSE

ery locations if possible. Allow at least 1 inch to square up the ends. Using the drawings, visualize the finished member within the rough timber. Remember that many pieces have a right and left version. You don't want to make two lefts! When you think you have positioned it properly, lay out the joint nearest the end. It isn't necessary to lay out every joint before you cut the first one, but it is important to know that one won't fall on a big knot. Lay out and cut the joint closest to an end first because if you make a mistake, there still may be enough timber length to move down a few inches and recut the joint.

The last thing before you begin cutting is to have a second person, if available, check the layout. If not, check it yourself. Remember to "measure twice and cut once."

When laying out a timber frame, try to think of it as a three-dimensional puzzle of sorts. You must be able to put those pieces together and visualize the house frame and its parts as you work. S.E. Todd, writing in 1870, put it nicely:

The builder, while laying out a frame, needs to set up a regular "air castle" before his imagination, so that he can perceive how every piece of timber, when he is laying it out, or framing it, will appear after the structure is raised and every part is in its proper place.

Each of the typical joints in the frame will be detailed in drawings and, for a few joints, I will take you step by step through the cutting process. It is *extremely* important to bear in mind that if there are right- and left-hand members, only one will be illustrated. The version that is not shown is a *mirror image* of the drawings.

Layout on Hand-Hewn Timbers. When the Square Rule was developed, most or all timbers were hand-hewn rather than sawn. When a timber was laid out, it was *lined* to the perfect inner timber with chalklines that were snapped on each face to delineate the planes of this inner timber. Since this system is also handy for bowed, twisted, or out-of-square timbers, I will discuss it briefly.

First, put the proposed best or reference face up. Shim the piece until this surface is generally level. If the layout lines from hewing are still visible, shim until these lines are level (or plumb, depending on the piece's orientation). Hold the tongue (or the blade with 2-inch tenon framing) of the square against the end of the timber flush with the top surface. Sight down this surface of the timber and move the tongue up or down until it appears flush with all the high spots of the uneven surface. Level the tongue of the square as you do this. Now, draw a line on the underside of the tongue. This line represents a plane inside the timber that is generally parallel with the high spots of the surface but lies 1½ inches below it. Turn the square so that the blade is flush with that line and the tongue is generally flush with the secondary reference face. Draw a line along the tongue perpendicular to the first line and 1½ inches away from the high spots of the surface. If the timber is out of square, it may only be flush along one edge of the second face. These two lines represent one side of the mortises or tenons. We need two more lines that represent the perfect inner timber. These lines are drawn with the level the desired distance from the other lines.

After repeating this procedure at the other end of the timber, snap two chalked

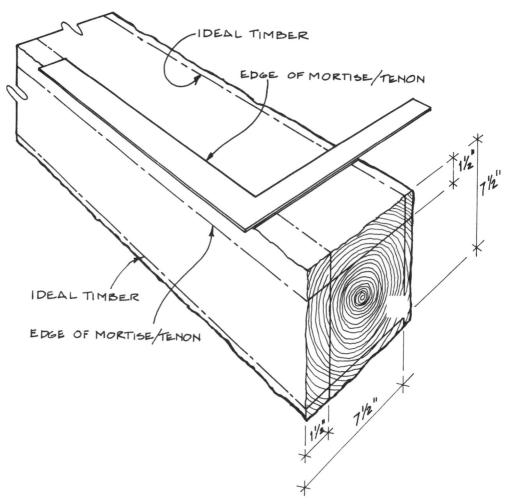

IDEAL TIMBER

EDGE OF MORTISE/TENON

1½"

7½"

IDEAL TIMBER

EDGE OF MORTISE/TENON

1½"   7½"

▲ *How to use the framing square and the chalked lines for layout on a "lined timber."*

lines on the top face where the two vertical lines meet the surface. Rotate the timber and repeat on each of the four faces. In general, a chalkline is most accurate when it is snapped vertically, so the plane it will define should be vertical. Since you cannot use a square against the edge of a hewn timber with any accuracy, all joinery is squared up by applying the inside edge of the framing square along the 1½-inch line. To layout a mortise or tenon, the tongue is laid with one edge on the chalked line and a line drawn on both sides of it. Housings are cut to the line that represents the perfect timber.

Chalked lines are typically a ¹⁄₁₆ inch or more in width — certainly more than a sharp pencil or scribe mark — but this need not affect the accuracy of your work if you follow the center of the chalkline when applying the square. If you are working outside, protect the chalked lines from rain.

Tools for Cutting Joints. There is always a tendency to think that the old way of doing anything must be harder, and that until modern times people worked extremely hard. When we see old tools in museums, we immediately think of hard, laborious work. Of course, this wasn't necessarily true. Once you are accustomed to working with hand tools that are properly sharpened and tuned, you will find that they work well and that the work is not hard. Since the craft of timber framing developed using only hand tools, hand tools are still the best way to cut traditional joints. There are many new power tools for timber framing, but too often the joinery is redesigned to enable the joints to be cut with those tools, and then these power tools are not doing traditional joinery. In addition, power tools may seem to make our work easier, but when you consider the extra hours you must work to earn the cash to purchase them you may be increasing your workload. My friend Tim Cahill stated the case eloquently in the October 25, 1981 *Berkshire Sampler:*

Power tools are fast, but that's all they are. They are no more accurate than hand tools. Their life support systems have to be toted around from place to place, so they are less convenient. When you cut and drill with electric tools, the noise and the vibration and the power act as a veil between you and your work. There ceases to be any relationship between the builder and the material then, and it's easier to care a little less.

The frame shown in this book was cut entirely with hand tools from timbers rough-sawn at local sawmills. Hand tools require only a small initial monetary investment when compared to power tools, which is especially important to an owner-builder who will probably build just one house frame. These are the recommended minimum tools for joint cutting:

A 26-inch 8-point crosscut saw.
This should be professionally sharpened and set; don't assume that a new saw is

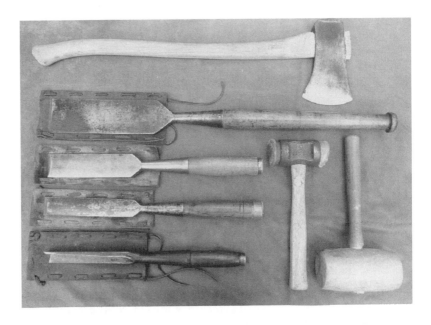

sharp. To keep it sharp, make a wooden slip-on blade guard.

An ax for roughing out joints. You can use one with a 32-inch handle, or choke up (place your hands farther up on the handle) on a longer one.

A 1½-inch socket framing chisel.
You need a heavy, thick, rugged chisel at least 15 inches long. Socket types are preferred to tang types as the handles last a lot longer and are easier to replace. The

▲ *Tools to cut joints (from the top): felling ax, slick, 2-inch chisel, 1½-inch chisel, corner chisel, and a rawhide-faced and a traditional wooden mallet.*

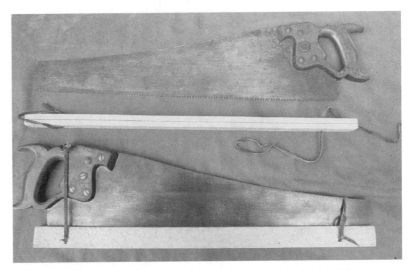

▲ *Hand saws should have wooden blade guards to protect the cutting teeth.*

▲ *Some new chisels that are readily available (from the top): A nineteenth-century chisel (with a new handle) for comparison, a socket framing chisel from Woodcraft Supply, and three Sorby tang-type chisels — extra long, bevel edged, and "Registered."*

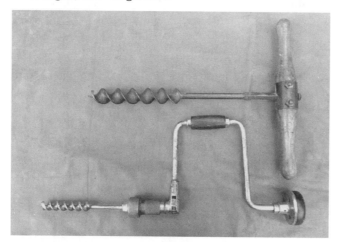

▲ *A T-auger (top) and a bit brace.*

chisel blade should preferably measure exactly 1½ inches but not more than 1/16 inch less. If it is exactly 1½ inches, you can use the blade as a gauge to check the width of mortises as you work. The back should have a slight convex sweep lengthwise, because if it is perfectly flat you will not have the proper control as you pare. The cutting edge should also have a slight curve to keep the corners from digging in. I prefer the old framing chisels when I can get them. They are usually stronger and heavier and most old chisels have a hardened steel cutting edge laminated to a mild steel body and socket. The cutting edge stays sharp and the chisel body absorbs the shock of mallet blows without breaking. Turned wooden handles with a ferrule prevent the head from mushrooming and fit into a socket in the chisel rather than over a tang.

A mallet for the chisel and pegs. I prefer a 2½-pound rawhide-faced mallet with a cast-iron head. Rawhide mallets make the chisel handles last longer and shock your hands less than some other types. Wooden mallets are fine as well and you can make them as the need arises.

A 1½-inch bit to bore out mortises. The simplest device to bore holes is a T-auger, but it is also the most time consuming. Prior to boring machines, T-augers were the most common boring tools. T-augers fit easily in the tool box, have no moving parts, are inexpensive, and can bore holes at any angle, even overhead. However, the boring machine is by far the best way to bore out mortises. At the time of this writing, antique tool dealers still offer them at prices below that of a good

◄ *Some boring machines (from the left): Millers Falls, Snell, and "The Boss" Double Eagle.*

BUILD A CLASSIC TIMBER-FRAMED HOUSE

power drill. Most models have depth stops, automatic returns, and can be set to bore perpendicular to the beam's surface. Unlike most power drills, boring machines have a set screw to keep the bit in the chuck, which is a necessary feature when boring deep holes. You sit or kneel on the base and crank the machine with both hands. Some have adjustable handles for more or less torque, and others have two chucks with different ratios, with the faster ratio presumably for smaller-diameter bits. Some models fold up for storage. I have been working with boring machines for over fourteen years and I think, considering all factors, boring machines are more efficient than power drills.

A $13/16$- or $7/8$-inch bit for boring peg holes. I use a bit brace to bore peg holes but you can also use a boring machine. Make sure you can bore a hole at least 8 inches deep and 10 inches is better.

The above tools are the minimum needed for this project. If you want to make your work easier, acquire these additional tools:

A chisel with a 2-inch blade. Some of the joints are cut more efficiently with a larger chisel, and another chisel size is useful for making identification marks.

A corner chisel, ¾ to 1 inch wide. Corner chisels can be handy, especially with hardwood mortises.

A 3- to 4-inch wide slick. This is a large, heavy paring tool that is pushed and not struck. Slicks remove lots of wood quickly. Yours should measure 27 to 35 inches long overall and like the chisels should have a slight curve on the back. This curvature allows you to hollow out scarfs and housings to allow for distortion after shrinkage.

A smoothing or rabbet plane, and,

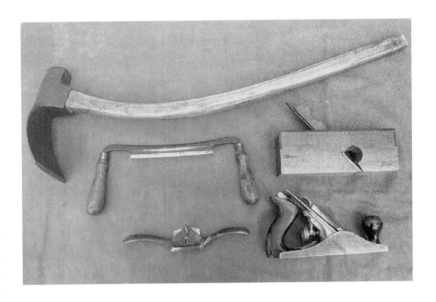

possibly, **a block plane.** A smoothing plane is useful for flattening tenons and smoothing surfaces. The rabbet plane allows you to plane tenons right up against the cheeks.

An adz. This multipurpose tool can rough out joints, scarfs, and smooth roughly hewn timbers. A short-handled adz can work a timber on sawhorses, but the longer ones are used with a timber on the ground or with the vertical faces of a timber on sawhorses. The head needs to be fairly heavy, with the back curved in both directions and a curved cutting edge. Shipwright's adzes and lipped adzes are lighter than carpenter's adzes but still usable.

A drawknife. Drawknives quickly remove the bark on waney edges.

A spokeshave. Spokeshaves smooth out waney edges and chamfer timber edges.

A 4- to 6-point 26-inch ripsaw. Depending on the straightness of the grain, it is sometimes faster to ripsaw the sides of a tenon.

A 2-inch auger bit for certain mortises and pockets would be a time-saver.

▲ *Shaping tools (clockwise from the top): adz, rabbet plane, smoothing plane, spokeshave, and drawknife.*

Sharpening Edge Tools

Dull or improperly sharpened hand tools quickly cause discouragement and frustration. A dull saw rapidly binds or makes it impossible to follow the cutting line. A dull chisel requires more effort and leaves a terrible finish. A dull auger or bit only bores under considerable pressure.

Saws. It is most important that you have properly sharpened and set crosscut and rip saws — there is a lot of sawing in timber framing. The right saw makes your work pleasurable. Have your saws sharpened by a professional first. In most areas there is someone that has a saw sharpening business that uses a filing machine that files all teeth to the same height and angle. These businesses usually also have jigs to set the teeth exactly, and a professional can adjust angles and tooth set for hard- or softwoods and green or dry wood; a good sharpener can even change the number of teeth (or points) per inch. For the small amount sharpeners charge, you can bring them your saws whenever they get dull. However, you may wish to file them yourself a few times in between machine sharpenings. If so, you will need to get a saw vise, files, a jointer, and a handset — see Payson (1988) in Further Reading.

Chisels. Chisels need to be properly tuned. Even new chisels need a little work! When looking for a chisel, look for one that is exactly or slightly less than 1½ or 2 inches wide with the sides parallel. A chisel more than 1/16 inch less than its intended width makes for extra work when cleaning mortises. The back of the chisel should have a gentle convex sweep along its length — approximately 1/16

inch. This sweep creates a pivot that allows you to control the amount you are paring off.

For sharpening, you only need two stones to get an edge that shaves hair: A combination course/fine India stone for general sharpening and a white Arkansas stone for the honing. The stones should be at least 2 inches by 6 inches but 8-inch long stones are better. For honing oil, I use a 1-to-1 mix of motor oil and kerosene, which is the least expensive honing oil you can buy. The Japanese water stones are an alternative popular among woodworkers, and they have their advantages and disadvantages. Water is free and readily available, but wipe down tools after sharpening with an oily cloth to keep them from rusting. The coarser Japanese stones do not cut as fast as India stones. The fine stones — 6000-grit and up — are excellent for honing, producing a mirror-finish, razor-sharp edge much quicker than the Arkansas stones. Unfortunately, they are soft and easily gouged by chisel corners.

Before you begin sharpening the bevel, work on the back of the chisel. All pitting, scratches, and other marks should be honed away until at least the first ¼ inch of the back has a mirror finish. Start with the India stone if the back looks badly pitted, then finish honing in a circular motion with the Arkansas stone. Any pits at the tip will create nicks in the cutting edge. It doesn't hurt if the back is slightly convex across its width, but it should not be concave. Now work on the bevel with the course stone to get the appropriate angle, which is approximately 30 degrees for softwoods and 35 degrees for hardwoods. These angles might vary depending on the specific softness of the wood you work, the hardness of the steel

BUILD A CLASSIC TIMBER-FRAMED HOUSE

in the cutting edge, and your personal preferences. Use a back-and-forth motion and considerable pressure. I also rock the chisel from side to side as I sharpen to make the bevel slightly convex across its width, creating a curved cutting edge (no more than about 3/32 inch) that keeps the corners of the chisel from digging in. Hold your chisel at a steady angle — use a honing guide if necessary — and grind the bevel until you feel a burr across the whole width of the cutting edge. Use lighter pressure for a few more strokes.

Once you feel the burr, switch to the fine stone. Hold the chisel at a slightly steeper angle (2 or 3 degrees) and only push it forward, lifting on the return stroke. This angle creates a microbevel. Use lighter pressure as you progress. The burr will eventually fall off as you hone, but you can also remove it by *backing off:* Lay the back of the chisel flat on the stone and pull the chisel toward you once, then wipe the stone and chisel to clear the steel fragments. Continue honing on the bevel with very light pressure until the edge has a mirror-finish microbevel and you can shave the hair on your arm.

Once the edge is sharp, you regularly need to touch it up by honing. After several honings, however, you need to sharpen the bevel again. With good steel and a sheath to protect the edge, you need only sharpen every couple of days. When your chisel stops leaving a smooth finish or has nicks in its edge, it is time to resharpen.

Other Tools. Sharpen plane blades like chisels. I have extra plane irons for my smoothing plane so that when one gets dull I can replace it with a sharp iron. When all of the irons are dull, I sharpen them at once to save setup time. Sharpen

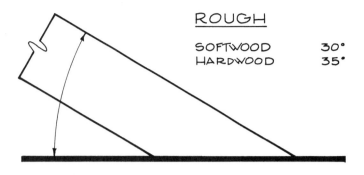

ROUGH

| SOFTWOOD | 30° |
| HARDWOOD | 35° |

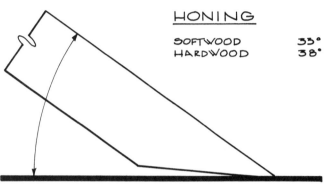

HONING

| SOFTWOOD | 35° |
| HARDWOOD | 38° |

CHISEL SHARPENING ANGLES

slicks like chisels, although you may need to turn the blade at an angle to fit it on a narrow stone. I use a shallower bevel angle for slicks as they aren't struck with a mallet. The corner chisels are sharpened on one edge at a time. Adjust the angle until only the top edge is touching the stone (the corner of the stone should be sharp, not rounded). Most old corner chisels are a little less than 90 degrees, which keeps the corners from digging in. For bits, I use fine files or small stones for sharpening. A file or India stone works fine when sharpening felling axes and broadaxes. Don't bother honing as the steel is too soft to hold the edge. Adz heads are taken off and sharpened like chisels except that the cutting edge should curve more convexly than a chisel — about 1/8 inch.

The Cutting Process

This section outlines the process of laying out and cutting individual joints. The instructions for the first few joints are very detailed and take you through all of the steps. I suggest that you begin with these joints before attempting some of the later, more difficult sections. It is also very important to remember that some of the members have both a right- and left-hand version and that only one version is shown; the other version will be its mirror image.

STUB MORTISE

The stub mortise is a very basic joint found where a post bears on the sill — a short tenon on the bottom of the post anchors the post on the sill. The joint is at one end of the piece, the top of the sill is the best or reference face (place that side up), and the exterior side of that face is the best edge. Put an arrow on the best face that points toward the best edge. After positioning the future timber within the piece, mark where your end cut should be. To draw your lines square around a timber, remember one important rule: The blade of the framing square can only be placed against the reference face or best edge (the secondary face). If you try squaring a line around successive sides, the lines probably won't meet unless the timber is planed to a consistent size. If you only square lines off of reference faces, they will meet, even on tapered pieces. First, draw your line across the top of the piece, then square the line down each side. There is no need to put a line across the bottom side.

Always begin sawing end cuts on the reference face so that any wandering will be less critical. Saw on the waste side of the line and take half the line with the cut. This may seem difficult to achieve, but it comes quickly with practice. Using your thumb as a guide, start the cut on the top face on the edge opposite you, which is the back edge. Cut only a shallow kerf — about ¼ inch — then bring your thumb to the edge nearest you (the front) and begin working the kerf toward you. Try to keep the saw in the whole kerf but don't advance any lower on the back face since you can't see the line there. When you have brought the kerf to the front edge, start down the front face. As you saw down, try to keep the saw in the whole top kerf, too. Continue sawing until the saw blade touches the top back and the bottom front edges — you have cut exactly halfway through on a diagonal. Walk

SILL CORNER STUB MORTISE

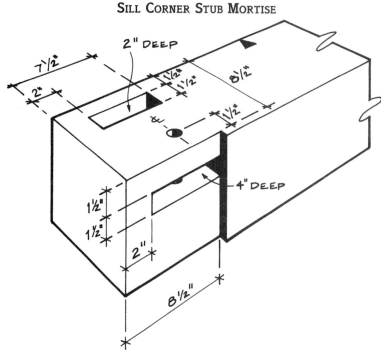

▲ *The large arrow on the reference face points towards the best edge.*

▲ Two lines are scribed off the best edge using a Japanese marking gauge.

▲ The ends are scored prior to boring with a light tap on the chisel.

▲ With the boring machine depth stop set for 2 inches, bore the two end holes first, then the two middle ones.

▲ The four holes should look like this.

▲ Pare down the sides of the mortise first and check them for plumb off the face with the combination square.

▲ The ends are squared with the corner chisel or the 1½-inch chisel.

around the timber. From the opposite side, keep your saw at least a couple of inches down in the previous cut and begin sawing down the face nearest you. As you approach the bottom, support the free end to keep it from falling prematurely; you may need to support it with a sawhorse or your upper leg.

Next, you will lay out the mortise's position. The 8-inch post is framed to 7½ inches, so measure in that distance from the end of the sill. As the mortise will have a 2-inch relish (in this case, *relish* is the wood left between the mortise and the end of the timber), measure that out, too. As an alternative, you can use the 2-inch blade of the framing square to both measure and square that line in one step. Scribe the sides of the mortise with a marking gauge, a combination square and pencil, or the 1½-inch tongue of the square applied twice. Finish marking the mortise by scratching diagonal lines from each corner to show what will be removed.

Before boring, the mortise edges need to be scored to prevent the bit from tearing the wood beyond the layout lines. You can use a knife or lightly strike a chisel laid on each edge line with a mallet. Marking gauges score the sides automatically as you scribe the mortise but you still need to do the ends with a chisel or knife.

Bore both ends of the mortise first. If you are using a boring machine, place it over the mortise and sight down the edge of the bit until it lines up with the sides and end of the mortise. Start boring until the bit just starts to cut. If you have a depth stop, set it for 2 inches (or slightly more) of travel. Otherwise, mark a pencil line somewhere on the carriage where you will stop. Some machines have ¼-inch gradu-

ations stamped on the uprights. After each end is bored, bore the remainder of the holes, overlapping them if possible. These holes may wander because there is no wood on one side of the hole, but wandering is less of a problem in the middle. Before I begin boring, I determine the number of overlapping holes needed. If there are five holes required, I'll bore the ends, a middle hole, and then the remaining two. With an odd number of holes, there can be equal wood on either side of the hole to prevent bit wandering.

After boring the mortise, you must clean it up by paring. The sides of the mortise are pared first. Put your chisel into the scored line and push down — the curved remnants are easily pared away. Remember to keep the flat side of the chisel against the wall of the mortise when paring and to keep paring until the mortise sides are perpendicular to the top (reference) surface and the mortise is 1½ inches wide. Check the width by sliding the tongue of the framing square back and forth. Finally, square the corners. You can use the corner chisel if you have one or a 1½-inch chisel and the mallet. Pare the ends until they are square with the top surface, too. Check for squareness using a combination square set for 2 inches.

Because stub mortises are not pegged, this mortise is done. The mortise is on a reference face, so there is no housing. You do, however, need to indicate its location with a Roman numeral a few inches away from the mortise, in the center of the timber and across the grain. Refer to the discussion on the numbering of pieces at the end of this chapter.

HOUSED MORTISE

See the measured drawing for the Lap Dovetail Tying Joint shown on pages 114 and 115.

When a mortise is in a nonreference face, it must be housed to the ideal timber, a situation that occurs throughout the frame. This section looks at a mortise in the underside of the plate for an end post. Lay out the mortise as in the previous example, but make measurements on the reference face and bring them around to the mortised face. In addition to the mortise, you must lay out the housing. The 10-inch depth of the plate is framed to 9½ inches at the housing. Set your combination square to 9½ inches and draw a line around the sides and end of the timber. Thus, the plate is reduced to 9½ inches over each post.

At the inside end of the mortise, make a saw cut down to the housing depth. The rest of the mortise is scored as before. The mortise depth is 4 inches beyond the housing, so add the housing depth to the overall depth. Because the housing depth can vary with the actual timber size and even along a timber, check the depth for each mortise. If the timber is exactly 10 inches, it would have a ½-inch housing, so the depth would be set at 4½ inches or a little deeper. When you set the boring machine up to bore on a nonreference face, check to see if that face is reasonably square with the reference face. If it isn't, shim the machine to compensate. The finished mortise should, of course, be perpendicular to the ideal timber.

After boring, clean up the sides first as before, but note that you cannot check the mortise sides for perpendicularity to the surface because it is not a reference face. Using the combination square and the framing square, you can check the sides off of the reference face. The ends, however, can be checked well enough off the surface. When the mortise is complete, cut out the housing. This is chisel-and-mallet work, although I sometimes rough it out with an ax. Work the edges down to the line, then cut the center. To create a surface that will be flat when the timber has seasoned, you must actually hollow the green timber, which is when the chisel or slick with a slightly curved back is necessary. On white pine, I hollow the shoulder between ¹⁄₁₆ inch and ⅛ inch, but use more for woods with higher shrinkage rates. Without this hollowing, there will be gaps when the timber dries.

To lay out the peg hole, turn the reference face up. Place the tongue of the square flush with the edge of the mortise and draw a line on the opposite side. Locate the center of the peg hole on this line in the middle of the mortise. With a bit brace, bore a peg hole until the bit just breaks through into the mortise. Before continuing, sight it from two directions to be sure it is vertical. Continue boring till the tip barely pokes through the bottom of the timber. Flip the timber over and finish boring out the remaining wafer-thin portion. Sometimes turning the bit backwards helps prevent tearouts.

▲ *The edge of the housing is sawn down to the shoulder, which simultaneously scores the ends of the mortise.*

▲ *Bore four holes to the depth of the mortise plus the depth of the housing, which should be about 4½ inches.*

▲ *The sides of the mortise can only be checked for plumb off of the reference face — use the combination square and the tongue of the framing square.*

▲ *The ends can be checked for plumb off of the surface.*

◄ *The housing should be scooped out towards the middle to allow for shrinkage.*

▶ *The finished mortise.*

GIRDING BEAM MORTISE

This joint has a through-mortise, and since the tenon enters on a nonreference face, you must house the joint. Since the girding beam is a nominal 10 inches re- duced to 9½ inches, the mortise mea- sures 9½ inches. The 8-inch post is framed to 7½ inches at the housing. Lay out on the reference face the 9-foot level

GIRDING BEAM MORTISE

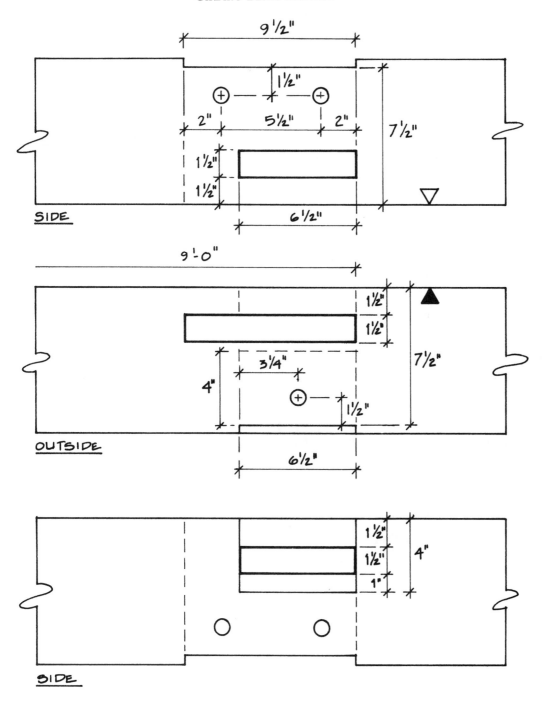

▲ *Both ends of the housing are sawn and seven holes are bored halfway through from each face.*

▲ *On these larger mortises, the slick is more effective for paring than a chisel.*

of the second floor level. Next, measure down 9½ inches to give you the other end of the mortise. Bring these lines around all four faces of the post. From the best edge, lay out the sides of the mortise as before on the shouldered face and the opposite face since through-mortises are cut halfway from each face.

Saw the ends of the mortise down to the housing depth and then score the mortise sides. On the outside reference face, just score the edges. Bore seven holes just past half the total depth from each face. The chisel work is done as with other mortises, but you do need to flip the post over periodically to work the mortise from both sides. The slick works especially well on the sides of this mortise. When you slip the tongue of the square in the finished ideal mortise, you should be able to slide it back and forth with only minor resistance. At the ends, it should touch the line at both the top and bottom faces and be nearly straight in between.

The housing is roughed out quickly with the ax. Bring down the ends first and then split off the sections between. You then use a slick or a chisel to pare to the line. Again, the housing must be hollowed out to allow for shrinkage distortion.

The mortises for the wall girts also occur at this level. On posts 2 and 3, one mortise intersects the through-mortise and the other comes very close to it. It would be wise to place a snug-fitting block in the through-mortise to prevent tearout when boring and chiseling these other mortises.

▲ *Check the width of the mortise by sliding the tongue of the framing square in the mortise.*

▲ *The ends are finished with a corner or 1½-inch chisel.*

◄ *The housing is quickly roughed out with the ax.*

▲ *The slick is also useful for paring the housing.*

▲ *Hollow out the housing toward the middle.*

All of this frame's brace mortises are in nonreference faces, so all will be housed to the ideal timber, a practice that was fairly common in old frames as the housing provided extra bearing. If I am laying out a plate, for example, I cut the post mortises before the brace mortises. Then I simply hook my tape measure on the shoulder edge of the post mortise and measure and mark 3 feet. Then I back up 7 inches for another mark. The 7-inch mortise length accommodates brace stock up to 5 5/16 inches wide. There is one exception to the 3-foot measure. Though the braces that go from the posts up to the tie beam are the same length and angle as the others, the joinery requires that the post brace mortise is measured 2 feet 7 inches from the shoulder. The tie beam brace mortise is measured out 3 feet 1½ inches. If you study the drawings, it will be evident why this is necessary.

Unlike the other mortises, the brace mortise has a housing on only one side.

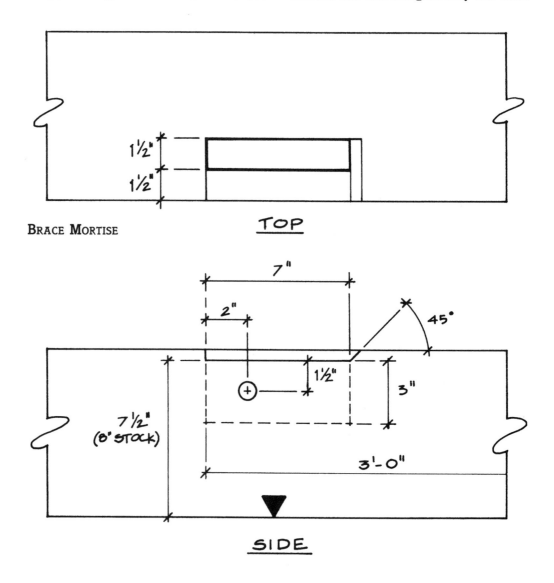

BRACE MORTISE

TOP

SIDE

The mortise measures 1½ inches in width and is 1½ inches from the face. The housing is measured from the reference face and is either 7½ inches for posts or 9½ inches for plates and girding beams. After the sides are scored, I score the ends by sawing down to the shoulder on an angle. Then I bore five holes 3 inches deeper than the housing.

After squaring up the mortise, I bevel the end opposite from the bearing end at a 45-degree angle to provide clearance. The peg hole is easily laid out using the square as shown. The hole is 1½ inches from the edge of the mortise and 2 inches from the bearing end.

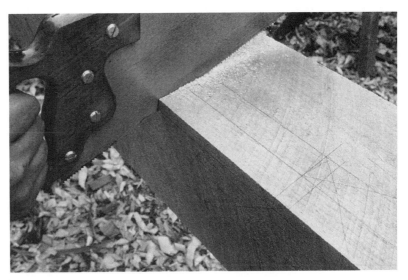

▲ *The housing can only be partially sawn.*

▲ *Bore the two ends and center of the mortise first.*

▲ *The peg hole is located by aligning the outside corner of the framing square against the square end of the mortise; scribe on the inside corner of the framing square.*

▲ *The finished brace mortise.*

You can see in the photos (see page 98) and drawings that this post top tenon occurs in a waney section of the post, but the wane is no problem. With the reference face up, lay out the 3⅞-inch long tenon. Using a drawknife, remove the bark and smooth the wane till it is flat. To drop the line down the vertical face past the wane, lay the blade of the square against the vertical face so the blade's edge lies flush with the top surface. Get down and sight across the blade or place a couple of heavy flat objects on the top surface and push the square against them. Now draw the vertical line. Lay your square across the wane and connect the two lines. Next, lay out the tenon on the end and sides of the timber. To measure down a waney edge for tenon layout, lay the edge of the blade on the top surface and mark where the respective marks on the tongue fall on the side of the timber. Connect these marks with the lines on the end of the timber.

Saw the shoulder, remembering that you are only sawing on the lines you can see. The waste on either side of the tenon can be split off with a mallet and chisel

INTERMEDIATE POST TOP TENON POSTS (BENTS 2 AND 3)

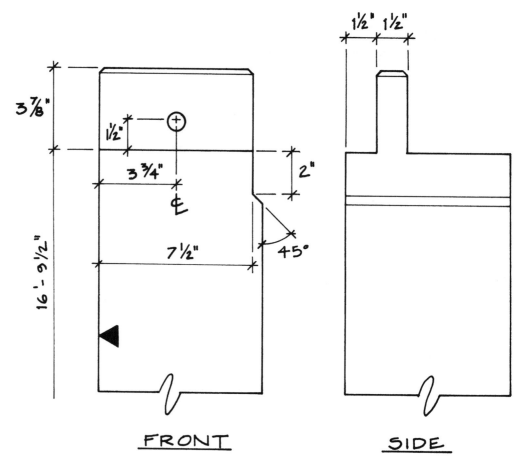

FRONT   SIDE

or an ax. Keep the chisel's bevel down for control and work your way slowly, splitting off about ⅜-inch chunks at a time. Watch the grain as you go down since if the grain wanders, the split could run below the line. When you are within ⅛ inch of the line, pare with the chisel or slick, working the edges to the line first. If you have a rabbet plane, you can plane the tenon to the line right up to the shoulder. When you have a flat tenon exactly to the line, taper the last 2 inches down about ¹/₁₆ inch. The taper won't affect the quality of the frame but does allow for easy insertion. The base of the tenon should be true, which you can check by applying the tongue of the square and feeling if it is flush with the surface.

Turn the timber over and draw a line that connects the lines on the sides. Saw down this shoulder. Because the waste here is much larger, you can split off chunks more aggressively but you still need to watch the direction of the grain. Pare to the line and again taper the tenon.

The tenon and top of the post must be reduced to the 7½-inch size where the tenon enters the mortise and housing. Set your combination square for 7½ inches and, using a pencil, mark a line all around the tenon and 2 inches down the post. Use the thickness of the blade of the framing square to mark the 2-inch line. Saw down along this line to the ideal timber. Split off the waste and pare to the line. With the chisel's bevel down and using the mallet, cut back the waste at about 45 degrees to create a bevel between the ideal inner timber and the rough outer timber. Make sure the last couple of inches of tenon on all four sides are tapered about ¹/₁₆ inch. The same tenon is

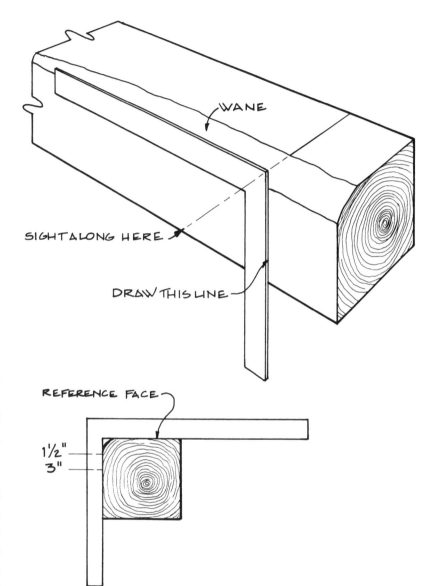

▲ *The square can be used on a waney edge by aligning the blade flush with the top (reference) surface. It can also be used to measure off of a waney corner by applying it as shown in the lower drawing.*

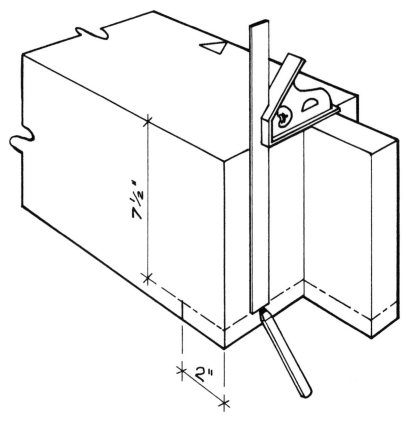

▲ *To lay out the 7½-inch post top, set the combination square for 7½ inches and mark all around the timber.*

used for single- and two-story posts. However, because of joinery conflicts in the sill girders, the basement posts can only have a 3-inch long tenon. If this were a corner post, on the other hand, one extra step would be necessary: Two inches of the tenon must be removed to allow for the relish on the mortise. Lay out this cut from the outside face of the post with the combination square set for 2 inches and then saw and chisel the waste. Taper as with the other sides of the tenon.

The ends of all the post tenons get a ¼-inch chamfer on the four edges by paring with a chisel held askew, which allows the chisel to slice through more easily. You could also use a plane held askew.

To lay out the peg hole, place the blade of the framing square against the best edge and the tongue on the tenon against the shoulder. Mark a line against the tongue that shows the distance from the shoulder. Find the center of the tenon (3¾ inches from either side) and mark a V there. Since we are drawpinning, bore about ⅛ inch closer to the shoulder, but don't mark this difference — just eyeball it and bore. When the point pokes through, finish the hole from the other side.

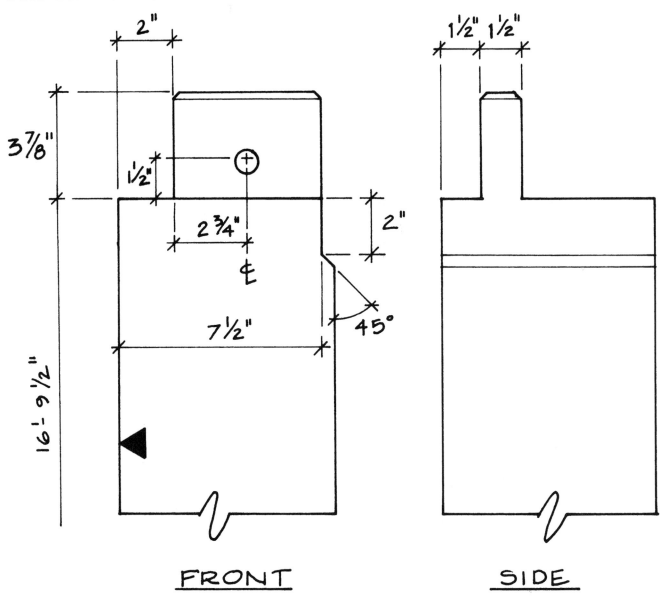

FRONT

SIDE

▲ *The posts of bents 1 and 4 are similar to the posts of bents 2 and 3 but have 2 inches of the tenon removed to provide relish in the mortise at the end of the plate.*

▲ *Connect the lines across the wane after you have squared down the side.*

▲ *The tenon is also connected across the wane.*

▲ *After the rough chisel work, the rabbet plane can smooth the tenon to the line right against the shoulder. Use the smoothing plane to finish the surface.*

▶ *The tenon can be checked by applying the tongue of the framing square against the shoulder — the square should be flush with the surface of the timber.*

▲ First, saw the side of the post and then chisel down to 7½-inches. The rabbet plane can be used here as well.

▲ Using the mallet and chisel, make a 45-degree bevel.

▲ To lay out the peg hole, align the tongue of the framing square against the shoulder and the blade against the best edge; scribe a line and then mark a V in the center of the tenon.

▲ The peg hole is offset towards the shoulder about ⅛ inch.

◀ The brace and bit bores a clean hole.

POST BOTTOM STUB TENON (BENTS 2 AND 3).

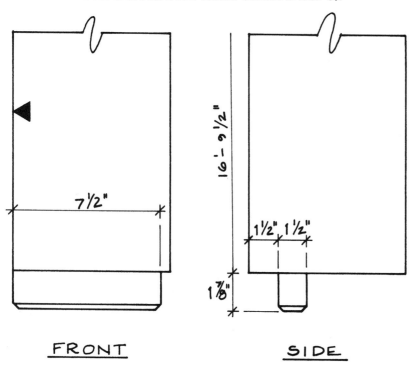

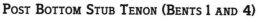

FRONT   SIDE

These tenons are similar to the post top tenons but are shorter because they only serve to locate the post in the sill. They are not pegged — only the tenon is reduced to the 7½-inch dimension as there is no housing on the top of the sill. The corner post stub tenons are cut down 2 inches in width to provide relish in the mortise. Give them a healthy taper and chamfer for easy insertion.

POST BOTTOM STUB TENON (BENTS 1 AND 4)

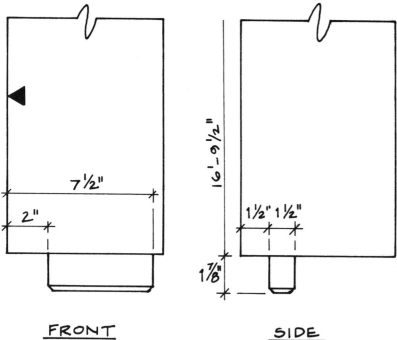

FRONT   SIDE

Sill Corner Tenon

These tenons are identical to the corner post top tenons except that they are framed in 8x9 stock.

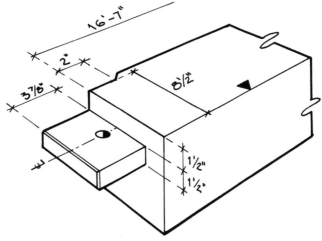

Sill Corner Tenon Layout

Girding Beam Tenon

This through-tenon is 7¼ inches long and worked much like the corner post top tenons. However, because of its size, you can use the ax to rough it out. For paring, the slick is indispensable here. Taper the last 2 inches or so of the tenon about 1⁄16 inch. The end of the girding beam and tenon get reduced to 9½ inches where they fit into the post mortise housing.

Because this is an important joint, it receives two peg holes. Lay the square on the tenon and mark a line along the tongue. Place a V-mark 2 inches in from each edge of the tenon.

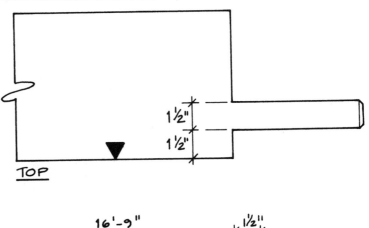

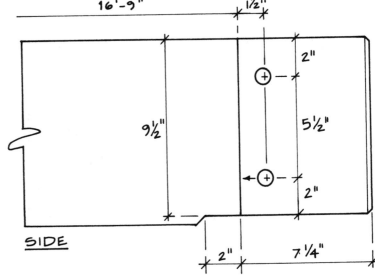

Girding Beam Tenon

▲ *Be careful when sawing down to the shoulder — only saw along the two lines you can see. Finish up by sawing from the opposite side.*

▲ *The ax can quickly rough out the tenon.*

▲ *The bottom of the beam is brought down to 9⅛ inches at the joint.*

▲ *The finished joint with peg holes and identification marks.*

SILL GIRDER MORTISE AND TENON

This joint is similar to the girding beam mortise discussed earlier but it is reduced in two dimensions as it joins the sill. The sill girder is not only reduced at the end to the 9½-inch width, but the depth is reduced to 6 inches. The housing on the sill is 6 inches instead of the full width. This provides bearing so all the weight is not on the tenon.

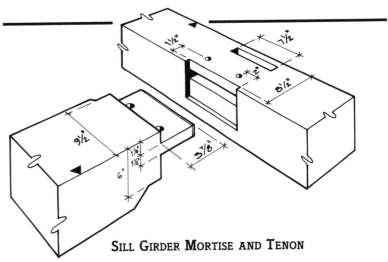

SILL GIRDER MORTISE AND TENON

BRACE TENON

Because the braces make the frame plumb, true, and resistant to racking, they are important elements. To many novice framers, making braces work seems like a formidable task. However, I hope to show you that if you use the Square Rule and cut to the line, braces are not difficult. When erected, the frame will be plumb and true. You may also find it useful to refer to the section on rafters that follows for drawings that show how to lay out pitches with a framing square. If you still have difficulty, however, *The Steel Square* (Siegele 1988) is an excellent reference — see Further Reading.

The length of the diagonal braces is determined from the Pythagorean theorem, which says that the square of the hypotenuse (the long side) of a right triangle is equal to the sum of the squares of the other two sides, which is usually written as $A^2 + B^2 = C^2$, where C is the hypotenuse. If the sides of our triangle (A and B) are 36 inches long — one of the more common sizes in the past — then our brace length is 50.9117 inches. Round that off to 50¹⁵⁄₁₆ inches. This number and other common brace sizes can be found in the brace tables on many framing squares.

BRACE TENON

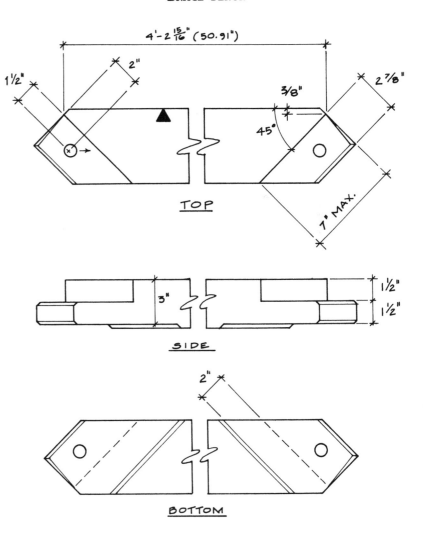

TOP

SIDE

BOTTOM

Two braces can be cut from a 10-foot long piece (3¼-inch by 5-inch stock). With the best face up, determine the best edge and make sure the edge is square with the face. Establish a reference line on the top face that is ⅜ inch from the best edge, which gives a ½-inch bearing shoulder that will approximately match our housing. On the other hand, if our housings were about 1 inch deep, then this distance would be ¾ inch instead. Regardless, set out this line with the combination square on a sawn timber or with a snapped chalkline on hewn or curved stock. All the brace angles are 45 degrees, so lay them out with the framing square as a 12-in-12 pitch off the best edge (or chalkline). Then the vertical lines are dropped square.

The first cut is the end of the tenon. Then, with the combination square, drop a vertical line on the cut face and then saw the nose or bearing end. Drop a vertical line again. Lay out both sides of the tenon all the way around and a few inches past the joint. Cut the shoulder line down to the tenon. Split off the chunks and pare to the line (the rabbet plane works well here). If the tenon grain is wavy or knotty, you may find it faster to ripsaw the tenon. Turn the brace on edge and saw only the two lines that you can see. Then flip it over and finish the cut. Touch the sides up with the chisel if necessary, then taper the tenon as before. Because it is a barefaced tenon (a shoulder on only one side), the other side merely gets taken down to the tenon. The end of the brace must be reduced to 3 inches thick a few inches back to clear the housing. If only $\frac{1}{16}$ inch or ⅛ inch needs to be removed, a plane is more appropriate than a chisel. If it is more than ⅛ inch, saw down to the line and pare it away. Don't forget to bevel it back as with the other joints. Chamfer all end-grain edges on the tenon.

If the brace stock is over $5\frac{5}{16}$ inches wide, the piece needs to be brought down some to fit the housing. Since the housing length is 7 inches, measure your shoulder to see if it is smaller. If more, reduce the width with an adz or plane. If it is less, there will be a gap at the nonbearing end of the mortise, but the gap does not affect the integrity of the frame and was standard in old frames.

The peg hole placement is easy. With the tongue of the square against the

$$36^2 + 36^2 = 50.91^2$$

7½"

9½"

36"

50.91

36"

THE MATHEMATICS OF BRACE LAYOUT

shoulder and the blade tight against the nose, scribe a line on the tenon. Scribe a V on the line 2 inches from the bearing end. When boring, offset the hole towards the shoulder but make it parallel with the piece, which will pull the joint tight. To lay out the other end of the brace, measure $50^{15}/_{16}$ inches from the point of the nose. All braces are interchangeable so there is no need to number them.

◀ *After cutting the end off, drop the line of the nose of the brace down the end and make this cut.*

▲ *Drop the shoulder line down with the combination square.*

▲ *Split off the waste wood as you would on any tenon and pare or plane to the line.*

▲ *Chamfer the end grain edges and bore the peg hole.*

▲ *Finished black cherry braces.*

▲ *When assembled, the brace should be snug at the bearing end. The gap at the far end of the joint is to allow stock of varying widths.*

These are pockets that the attic joists merely drop into. Saw the sides of each pocket down to the line as shown. In softwoods, they can then be worked down with a chisel and mallet. In hardwoods, it may be faster to bore the hole. If you are using the chisel, first split out the triangular waste chunk. Then, starting at the top, work the three vertical faces down together. Check with the combination square as you do. When you get to the bottom, work carefully as you do not want to undercut the weight-bearing part of the pocket. To check the bottom, set your combination square for 4½ inches, using the top as a reference.

If you bore these pockets, use a 1½- or 2-inch bit and remember to score the edges of the mortise with a chisel to prevent tearout and to set your depth at about 4¼ inches. You may want to bore before you saw since with some woods the blocks might split out as you bore. The corner chisel effectively works the corners.

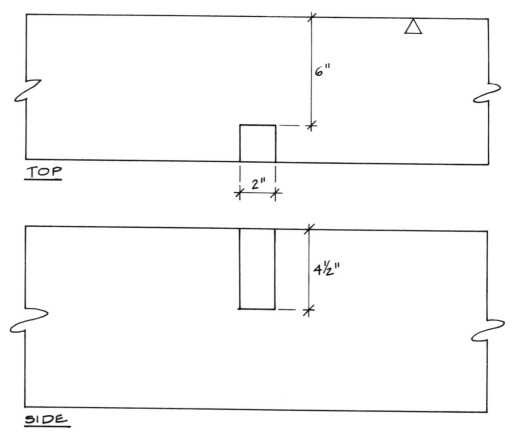

TOP

6"

2"

SIDE

4½"

ATTIC JOIST POCKET

▲ *The pockets are easier to saw if you lay the plate down flat. Saw until you just touch each line.*

▲ *The triangle of waste wood splits off easily.*

▲ *Work down the vertical faces but keep square with the top.*

▲ *The last bit of waste is scored all around from above and then split out from the side.*

◀ *Set the combination square for 4½ inches and check the depth and squareness of the sides.*

The first-floor joist pockets are worked similarly to the attic joist pockets, but because they are larger, boring definitely saves time. Bore two holes — one in each corner — to within ¼ inch of the pocket depth. The large triangular block is split out and the chisel is used as before.

The second-floor joist pockets have a housing of about ½ inch. The pockets in the center bay are also housed for strength even though they are in a reference face. After cutting out the upper portion, lay out the lower housing. For pockets on a nonreference face in the outer bays, drop vertical lines down from the top to locate the housing. For pockets in those bays in a reference face, set your combination square for ½ inch and mark off the face. The housing is sawed and chiseled out.

The tying joist mortises are similar to the previous mortises. After layout, the housing is sawed and the mortise is scored and bored. After the mortise is finished, the housing is chiseled out. Check it for square off the top (reference) face.

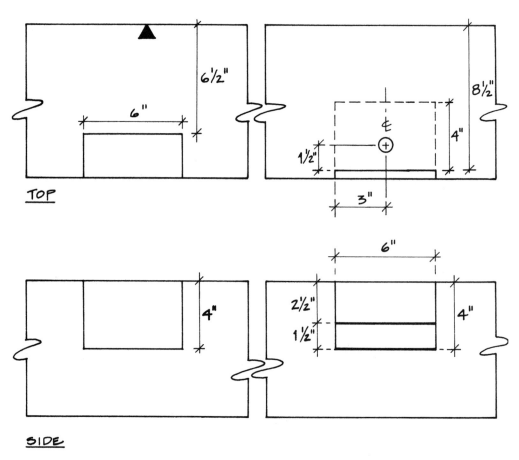

FIRST-FLOOR JOIST POCKET (END SILLS, 8x9 STOCK)

FIRST-FLOOR JOIST POCKET (IMTERMEDIATE SILL, 8x10 STOCK)

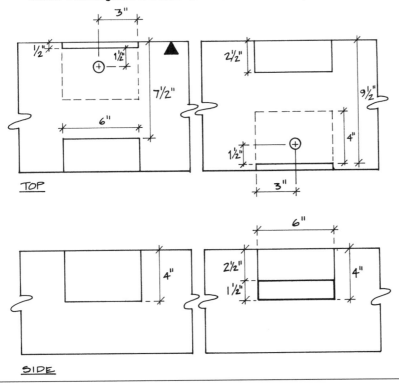

SECOND-FLOOR JOIST POCKET (GIRDING BEAM, 8x10 STOCK)

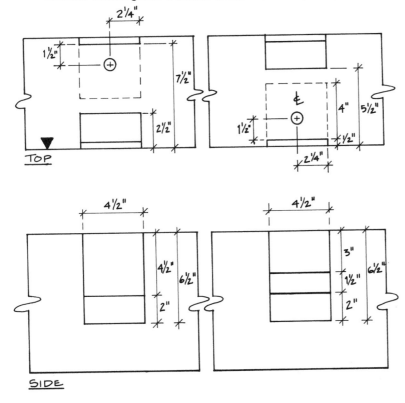

▲ *Drop-in joists.*

The drop-in joists are fairly simple. Square them to length and lay out the ends. You can choose to saw them out entirely or to saw and chisel them. Traditionally, the joists were not sawed at all. They were roughed out with an ax while upside down in their pockets. They were adzed flush with the sill and the bevel was dressed with the adz. If they are thicker than 6 inches, the joists have to be planed down to fit. Tying joists are similar to drop-in joists but have their tops cut to create a barefaced tenon, which has a shoulder on only one side.

FIRST-FLOOR DROP-IN JOIST

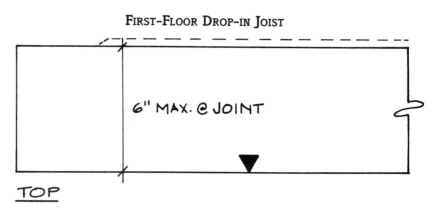

6" MAX. @ JOINT

TOP

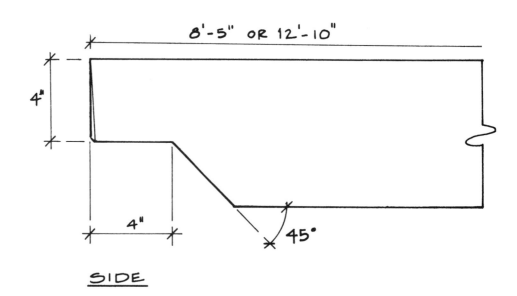

8'-5" OR 12'-10"

4"

4"

45°

SIDE

◀ *Tying joist.*

FIRST-FLOOR TYING JOIST

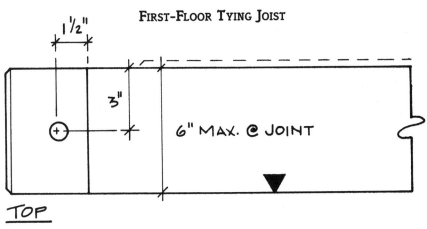

1½"

3"

6" MAX. @ JOINT

TOP

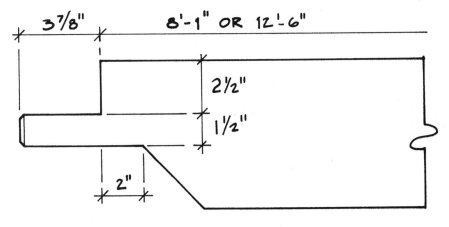

3⅞"

8'-1" OR 12'-6"

2½"

1½"

2"

SIDE

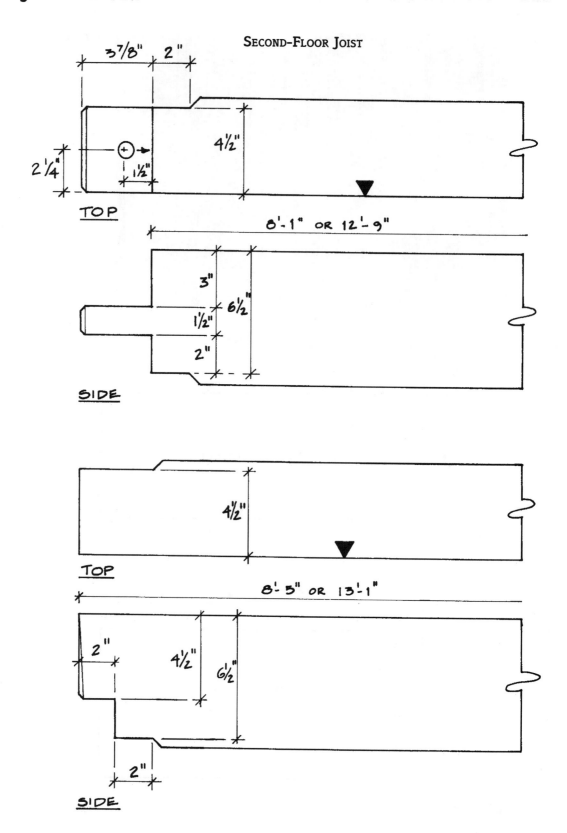

SECOND-FLOOR JOIST

3 7/8"   2"

2 1/4"

1 1/2"

4 1/2"

TOP

8'-1" OR 12'-9"

3"

6 1/2"

1/2"

2"

SIDE

4 1/2"

TOP

8'-5" OR 13'-1"

2"

4 1/2"

6 1/2"

2"

SIDE

Second-Floor Joist and Girt (continued)

The drop-in joists are relatively easy. The whole joist end is housed into the girding beam, so reduce it to 4½ inches wide by 6½ inches high at the end. The tying joist tenon is cut like other tenons.

In effect, the girts in this frame are floor joists against the outside wall, although they do join to the posts. The two girts in the center bay have stub tenons — in this case only 1⅜ inches long — and are not housed into the posts. Only the tenon has to be reduced to 6½ inches, but you might reduce the whole end to match the other girts.

SECOND-FLOOR GIRT

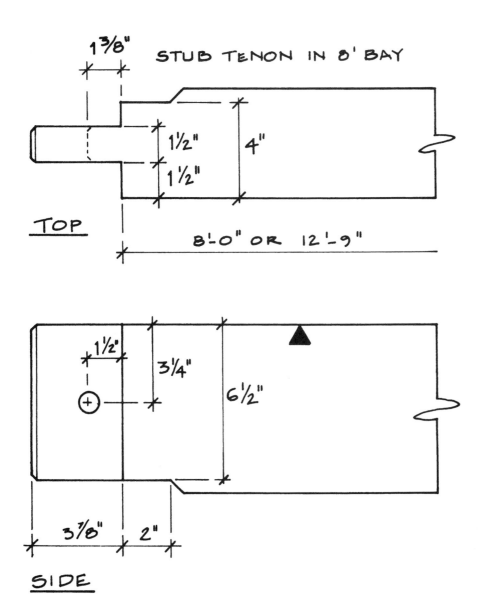

LAYING OUT AND CUTTING TIMBERS

LAP DOVETAIL (BENTS 1 AND 4)

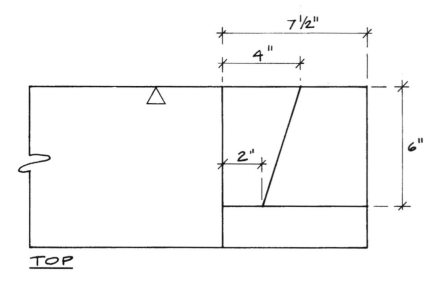

TOP

In order to provide relish on the ends of the plate, the end tying joints are different from the middle ones, but both are worked similarly. Cut the housing first, like it was a joist pocket. You can bore the housing or rough it out with an ax by standing on the plate.

Lay out the 2-inch deep dovetail on the side of the housing. The dovetail is sawed on either side and the middle is chopped out with the ax. Finish by paring to create a hollow to allow for shrinkage distortion.

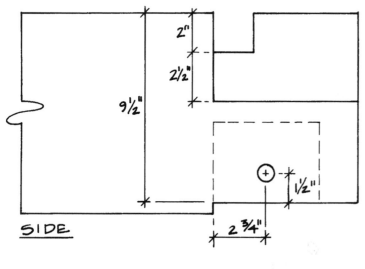

SIDE

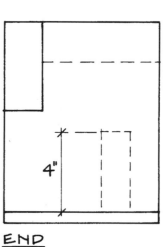

END

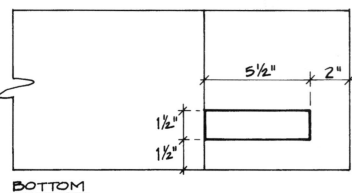

BOTTOM

Lap Dovetail (Bents 2 and 3)

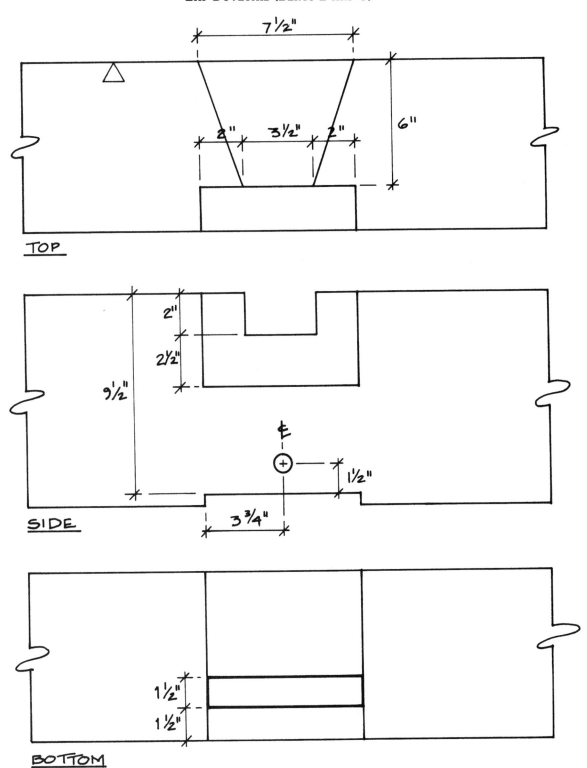

TOP

SIDE

BOTTOM

▲ *The housing is first cut out by sawing and chiseling. Be sure to check the accuracy of the depth and the squareness of your cut.*

▲ *With the combination square set for 2 inches, draw the bottom of the lap dovetail.*

▲ *Saw down the sides of the dovetail.*

▲ *Remove the waste with the ax and pare to the lines.*

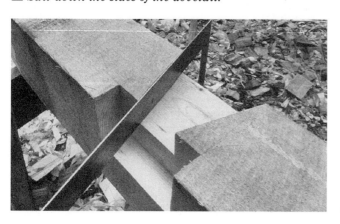

◀ *Check the depth by laying the blade of the square to see if it is flush.*

BUILD A CLASSIC TIMBER-FRAMED HOUSE

Finished Lap Dovetails

Tie Beam

These tie beams have considerable work in them and should be attempted only after you have gained experience on the other joints. There are two different dovetail designs, one for the ends and the other for the interior beams. Though the layout is a bit different, the procedure for cutting them is basically the same.

After squaring the end, cut out the 18-inch long lap portion by sawing down to the line at one or more locations. An ax can remove this bulk of wood quickly, but be sure the end is supported underneath by a sawhorse because the ax blows might otherwise cause a fracture. Score and split off chunks as with hewing. When you have split to within ¼ inch of the line, finish with a slick and a plane. This surface gets hollowed out about ⅛ inch.

Lay out the dovetail as shown. Saw down diagonally as with joist pockets. You can even bore out the corners if it saves

you time. Remember that this joint needs careful chisel work — this joint must be cut to close tolerances or it won't go together. When the dovetail is complete, the two nonreference sides must be brought down to the ideal timber size and beveled back. The rafter mortise on the top side is straightforward. There is no housing because it enters a reference face.

TIE BEAM (BENTS 1 AND 4)

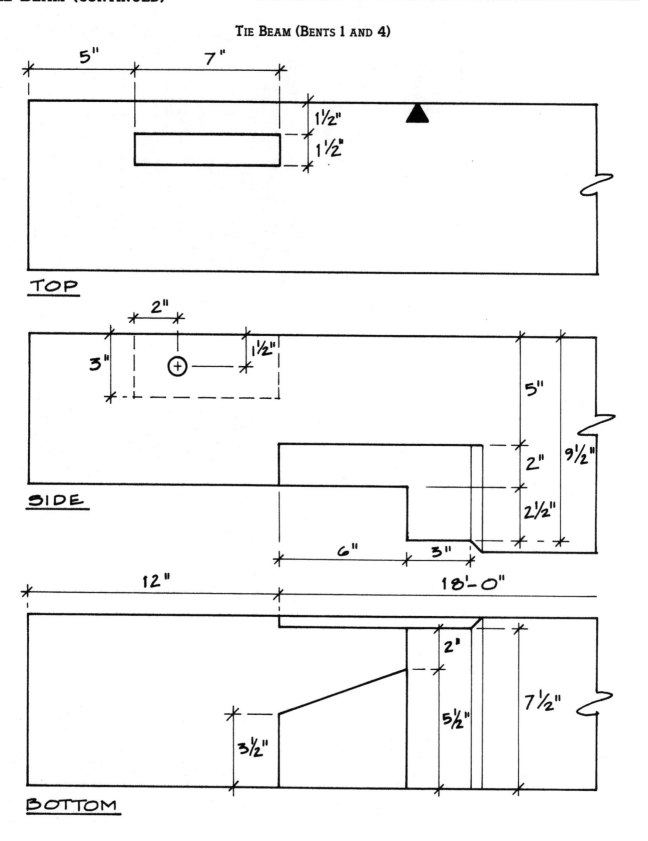

TOP

SIDE

BOTTOM

BUILD A CLASSIC TIMBER-FRAMED HOUSE

TIE BEAM (BENTS 2 AND 3)

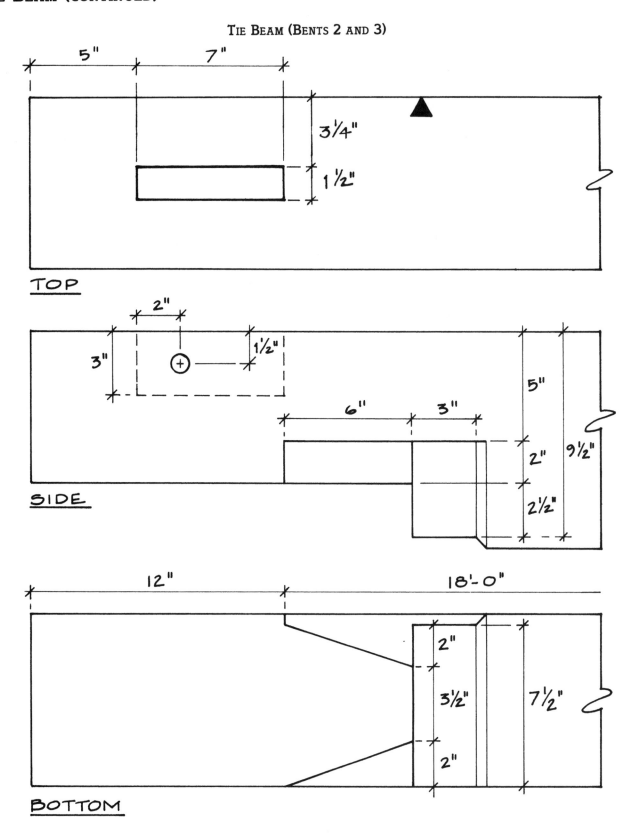

TOP

SIDE

BOTTOM

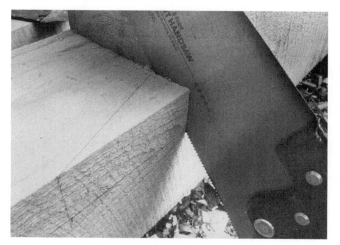

▲ *The dovetails are sawn first.*

▲ *The dovetails can be bored if it makes the work easier.*

▲ *The last step is bringing the tie beam down in thickness where it fits in the plate. Here is a finished tie beam from bent 2 or 3.*

▲ *An end tie beam for bents 1 or 4.*

Scarfs

Scarf joints that fit tight always gain the respect of onlookers. They are not that difficult to master if you follow these guidelines. When you lay out a plate or sill, put the scarf in the end that is the strongest and least waney and has the clearest grain, which is usually the butt or stump end. Be sure to pick the straightest edge for a reference, which can be hard with long timbers since they sometimes take a slight turn at the end. Lay out both upper and lower halves of the scarf from the top (reference face) and outside (best edge). That way, when the parts are assembled, they will be flush on those two faces. Inside faces may not be flush if the timber sizes differ, but they

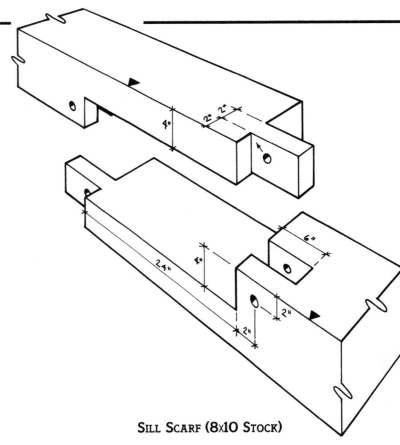

SILL SCARF (8x10 STOCK)

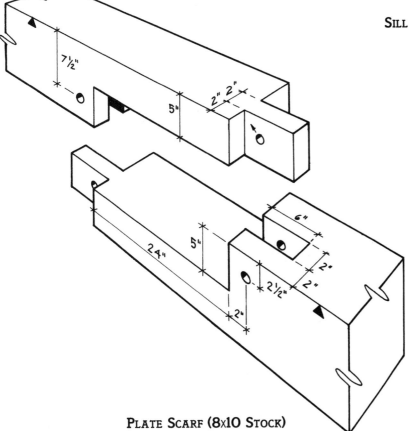

PLATE SCARF (8x10 STOCK)

can be planed flush if you don't like the way the variation looks.

Regardless, measure carefully and keep your pencil lines thin. Square up the end first before laying out the scarf. Mark the waste, which on one piece is the upper half and on the other piece is the lower half. Cut down to the 30-inch long half-lap. If the grain is knotty or wavy, saw at intervals of 4 inches. You could use a coarse fast-cutting crosscut saw here, but stay ⅛ inch from the line. Support the half-lap with a sawhorse directly under the middle of the joint and rough out with an ax. Pare to the line with a slick and a hand plane. Hollow it out at least ⅛ inch and more on the wider sill.

Finish laying out the mortise-and-tenon lines. Bore out and finish the mortise as with previous mortises. Three 2-inch holes will be sufficient. The bottom of the mortise should match the hollow of the half-lap. Undercut the end of the

mortise slightly. The tenon is cut as with previous tenons and remember to chamfer those tenon edges not exposed in the assembled scarf.

If you complete each half of the plate including the scarfs before fitting, you are taking a chance — you can't shorten a plate to make a better fit. I recommend that you complete only one plate half, including the scarf, without boring the peg hole in the scarf tenon. Cut only the scarf of the second beam, boring just the mortise peg hole. Assemble the scarf and shim the assembly until sighting down the edge reveals a straight timber, or if each has a crown, then at least a smooth transition. If things don't fit properly, mark where wood needs to be removed and take the beams apart. A pair of dividers set for the maximum gap can be used to mark all around. If the scarf is tight, mark the tenon peg hole placement by inserting an auger bit into the hole and turning it backward. Thus, only the point will pierce the tenon. Pull the joint apart enough to bore the tenon peg hole. Offset the hole as shown (add to the offset if the joint wasn't tight when the tenon was marked). The diagonal offset pulls the halves together vertically as well as horizontally. Put the joint back together and tap some pegs in to bring it tight, but use pegs with blunt points so that they can be easily driven back out, or try an iron hook pin.

With the halves properly fitted, a tape can be stretched down the entire length to lay out the rest of the joints. If your tape isn't long enough, put a good mark at 20 feet and move the tape to complete the layout and then disassemble the scarf and cut the joints.

▲ *Cut the lap portion first and hollow it out at least ⅛ inch.*

◀ *Bore three 2-inch holes in the mortise and finish with the chisel.*

◀ *Put the halves of the scarf together with removable iron hook pins to test the fit.*

◀ *Here is the sill scarf in position.*

These are quick joints that mostly require sawing. Because they are only 2 inches thick, the sawing is not laborious. The joists need only be laid out on one side, but check all cuts for squareness. One portion of waste has to be split out from one side, so support this area with a block or sawhorse below. Drive the chisel at an angle and stay ½ inch away from the line to avoid undercutting. These joists fit into 2-inch wide pockets. If the stock is thicker, reduce it as necessary just at the joint.

The framing for the chimney/attic hatchway can be mortised and tenoned as shown, or it can be a conventionally framed opening that is butted and nailed. I use nails to secure the joinery as the stock is too narrow to permit pegging.

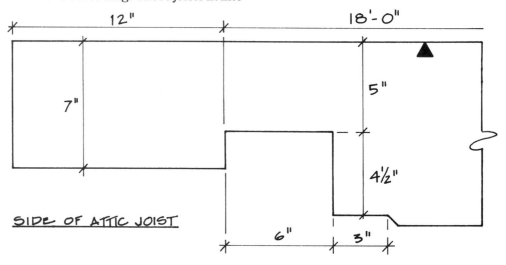

ATTIC JOIST

▲ *The waste block is split out with the chisel at an angle. Stay ½ inch away from the line to avoid undercutting.*

▲ *The finished joist end.*

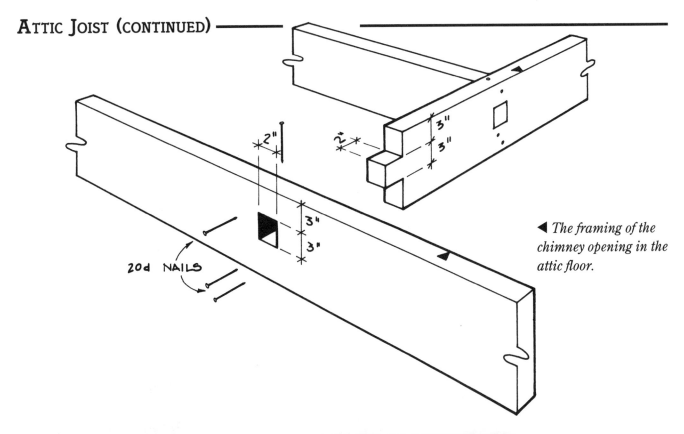

2"

3"
3"

20d NAILS

2"
3"
3"

◀ *The framing of the chimney opening in the attic floor.*

▲ *Here is the assembled chimney opening framing.*

With the exception of the east gable rafter pair, all the rafters are framed from the west. That is, their reference faces need to face west. The peak joint is an open mortise and tenon with the north rafters having the mortises and the south rafters having the tenons. Four rafter pairs are mortised into the tie beams to create trusses — which are rigid triangular assemblies — over each bent. The other rafters, which are intermediate or common rafters, are level-cut at the bottom and merely spiked down to the raising or false plate. Because they sit up 2 inches on this raising plate, they are shorter in length than the truss rafters. In some old structures, all the rafters sat on the raising plate and were nailed. The straightest pieces should be reserved for the gables, but crowns and bows are fine for the rest of the rafters.

Though the rafters are tapered, the layout is straightforward as you reference from only the best face and edge. As long as the rafters are at least 4½ inches wide at the peak for the joint, the taper doesn't matter. To lay out the peak joint, however, you need to figure the angle, which is based on the roof pitch of 9-in-12. Finding the angle that the rafter makes with its mate is a two-step process. On a wide board or piece of cardboard or plywood — possibly even your shop floor — lay out your 9-in-12 plumb line off a straightedge. This is the angle where a conventionally framed rafter would be cut to butt a ridgeboard. Lay out another 9-in-12 pitch off this line (you can use any measurement in the same ratio, such as 3-in-4, 6-in-8, 7½-in-10, and so on). This is our rafters' angle. If you have a bevel square, set it for the angle this line makes with the straight edge. You can also use the framing square and determine what number in-12 it is, which in our 9-in-12 pitch is 3½-in-12. Use this angle for all the peaks. The lengths all have to be figured with the Pythagorean theorem (see the section on braces earlier in this chapter). Note that the tenon at the peak is ⅛ inch short to allow for shrinkage.

Sawing the long angle cut at the foot is tedious and the saw often wanders on such cuts. Touch up the cut with a plane as necessary. The tenons at the foot are cut similar to braces but have a shoulder on either side. Saw out the notch first, then lay out and cut the tenon.

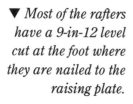

▶ *The rafters are reduced to 4½ inches where they join at the peak in an open mortise-and-tenon joint.*

▼ *Most of the rafters have a 9-in-12 level cut at the foot where they are nailed to the raising plate.*

TRUSS RAFTERS

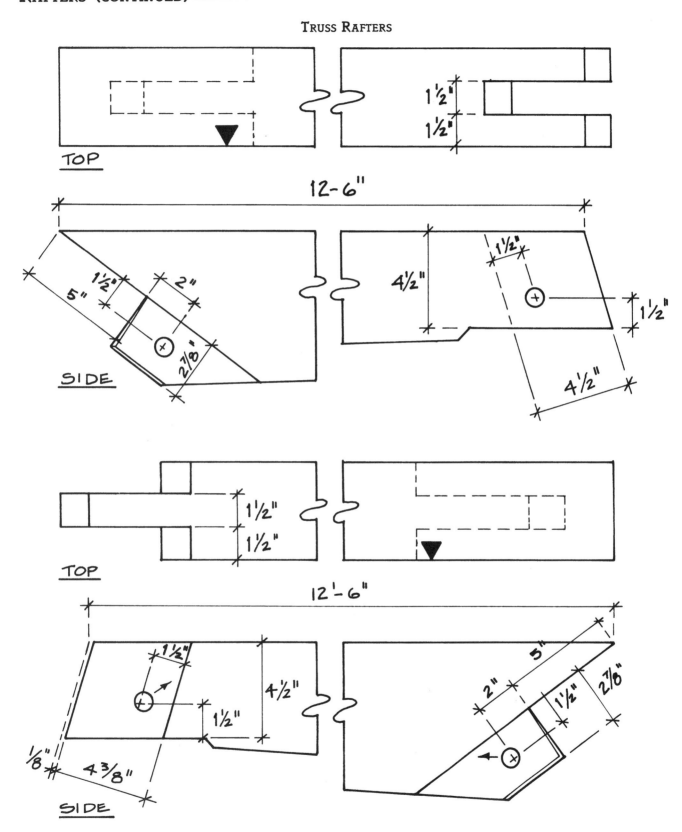

TOP

SIDE

TOP

SIDE

12-6"

12'-6"

INTERMEDIATE COMMON RAFTERS

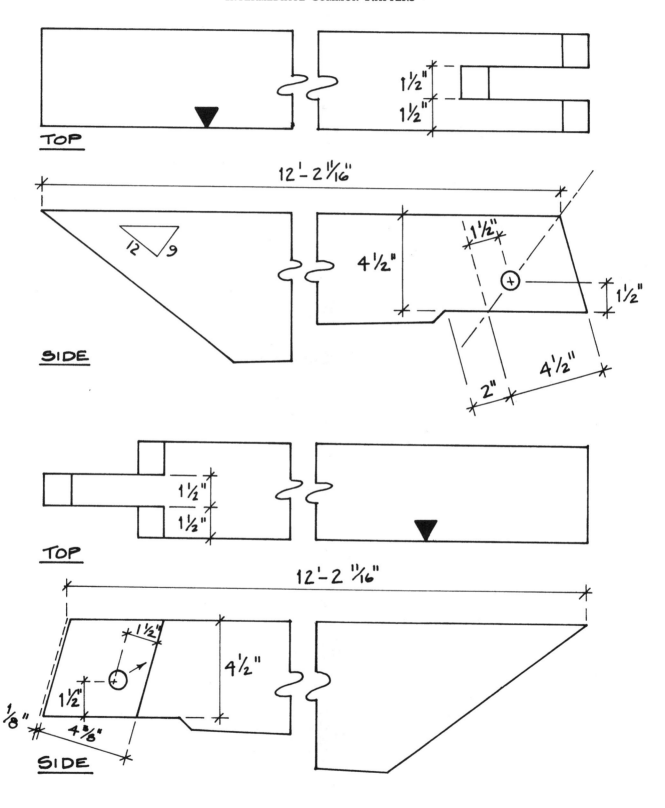

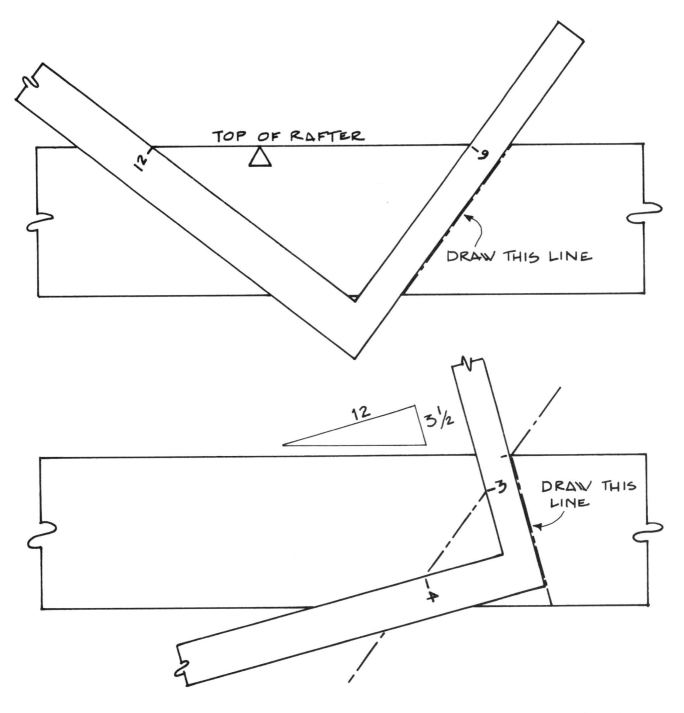

TOP OF RAFTER

12

9

DRAW THIS LINE

12

3½

3

DRAW THIS LINE

4

▲ *Laying out the peak angle. First lay out a 9-in-12 plumb line at the peak. Then, lay out another 9-in-12 (or similarly proportioned) line off the plumb line. This second step is best done on a wide board to be accurate. Record the angle with a bevel square.*

Planing and Chamfers

When each timber is finished, I usually take a plane to chamfer (bevel) each edge of the timber. A ¹⁄₁₆-inch chamfer softens any sharp, ragged edges. On waney timber, I remove the bark with a drawknife or chisel and spokeshave it smooth and uniform. If you don't like the rough-sawn surface, you can also plane the exposed faces. To prevent tearout of grain, I use a smoothing plane with a slightly rounded iron and push the plane diagonally across the face in a slicing motion. Planing lengthwise in the direction of movement is more likely to cause tearout. You should plane reference faces that are exposed before you lay out, because otherwise you are reducing the thickness slightly and the joints may be less tight.

In many early house frames, builders added decorative stop chamfers, which taper at one or both ends. These dressed up the frame and made it more user-friendly. In more expensive European frames, a lot of carving work embellished the frame. Here in America, frames were less fancy. By the time the Square Rule became popular, frames were no longer exposed on house interiors except in attics and cellars. Thus, there are very few (if any) old Square Rule frames with stop chamfers. Though it is a peculiar marriage, I sometimes use them. Mine are 1½ inches wide and the stop is 4 inches from the joint. The curved stop has ¼-inch reveal, a style that was probably the most popular as it was attractive, yet easy to cut. A line was drawn on each exposed corner that was 1 inch from the edge on either face. A saw kerf was made at each end, 4 inches from the joint, down to these lines. The wood in between the kerfs was scored with an ax, pared with a slick, and finished with a plane to the lines. The ends were cut back 2 inches in a graceful curve to leave the ¼-inch reveal. These curves are quickly cut with a chisel.

The post at the foot of the stairs, shown opposite, being a sort of turning point, was chamfered to make it octagonal, with stops that were beveled back rather than curved. This post could also be turned on a makeshift lathe to create a decorative newel post. A better solution is to select a smooth 8-inch diameter log, strip its bark carefully, and frame it as a post.

▶ *Ornate carving was fairly common in English villages.*

▶ *Stop chamfers dress up a frame. This simple yet attractive stop chamfer was chosen for our project house frame.*

▲ *Support the timber at a 45-degree angle and lightly score it with an ax every two or three inches.*

▲ *Pare to the line with a slick and smooth with a plane.*

▲ *Cut the curve carefully with a chisel, bevel down. Leave a reveal of about ¼ inch.*

▲ *The finished stop on a maple timber.*

▲ *An octagonal stair post.*

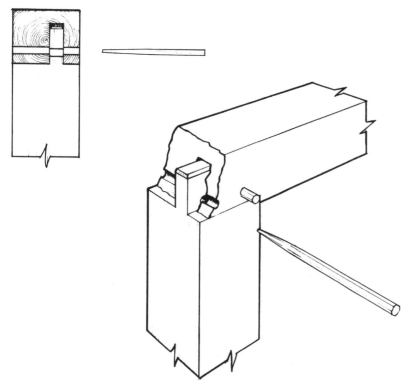

▲ *How drawboring works.*

▲ *The billet is marked into four-peg squares. With a froe and heavy mallet, keep splitting the billet in half.*

Pegs

Sometimes referred to as *pins, trunnels,* or *treenails* in old writings, pegs are an important part of the system. They draw and hold joints together. In most old frames, pegs were octagonal in cross section and tapered to a blunt, square point. By driving a tapered peg through offset holes, the joint was brought tight without other mechanical aids. In fact, this drawpinning system would keep joints tight during the racking of assembly and even after shrinkage. It may seem easier to bore the peg holes after the frame is assembled and pull the joints tight with come-alongs, but it isn't — it is a lot more work and the joints won't stay tight! If you use the traditional drawpinning system, all peg holes are bored as the timbers are worked, you won't be boring holes up in the frame later, and you shouldn't need any come-alongs, either.

Pegs are quickly riven or split out of freshly cut billets of a straight-grained clear hardwood. Cut the billets 4 inches longer than the deepest peg holes. In this frame, most pegs should be 12 to 14 inches long, with the pegs securing the rafter peaks measuring about 8 inches long (I've used $^{13}/_{16}$-inch diameter pegs, but $^7/_8$-inch ones are all right). On the end diameter of the billet, lay out a grid of $1^9/_{16}$-inch squares for $^{13}/_{16}$-inch wide pegs (or $1^{11}/_{16}$-inch squares for $^7/_8$-inch wide pegs). Using the froe and a froe club, first split the billet into quarters, and then split each quarter into two peg-wide sections. The most important principle of riving is that the split follows the grain if there is roughly equal wood on either side. If not, the split runs toward the narrower side. Thus, when riving peg blanks, you should be continually halving the sections until

▲ *Keep riving down to a square, split those squares in half, and then split those in half again.*

▲ *You should be left with straight, even, and square stock.*

you have a blank approximately $13/16$ inch (⅞ inch) square that exactly follows the grain. If you encounter knots, wavy or curved grain, or sapwood, throw the piece in the firewood pile.

Pegs should be shaped while still green or you will work a lot harder. They can be shaped with a shaving horse and drawknife if you have them. I use a jig to hold the blanks while I use a chisel and hand plane to shape them. My jig is a board with a V-shaped slot to hold the peg with a small block under the board to keep it from sliding. First, put a 3- or 4-inch long tapered point on the end opposite the layout end. Hold the blank with one hand and pare with a chisel in the other. Then hold the point end and pare the four edges off to create an eight-sided peg. If the blank was accurately split to size, you will end up with a peg that has alternate riven and pared faces within a couple of minutes. For a straighter, more uniform peg, use a block plane instead of or after the chisel. When finished, the distance across the flats of the octagon

▲ *You need to make a simple board jig to shape the pegs with slots to hold the pegs and a couple of holes to check the fit of the finished pegs.*

▲ *Pegs are held in one hand and shaped with a chisel or plane in the other.*

should be slightly less (1/32 inch) than the peg hole diameter and the distance across the corners of the octagon should be slightly greater than the hole diameter. Thus, when the peg shrinks, its corners should still dig into the sides of the hole. Because each peg will be driven through offset holes, however, it is not the fit of the peg in the hole that makes the joint tight. Allow a couple of weeks of drying time before using. Green pegs mash or split easily when driven and, of course, shrink and loosen.

In a couple of late nineteenth- and early twentieth-century frames, I have found lathe-turned pegs. Obviously, the builder had access to a woodworking shop. But turned pegs weren't common. Today, many framers are using turned pegs. For strength and appearance, I still prefer riven, hand-shaved, octagonal pegs.

Peg holes were laid out with the framing square as a template, which is necessary for proper drawboring/drawpinning. Most peg holes are 1½ inch off the shoulder of the joint. The mortised peg hole is bored right on the mark, but the tenon peg hole is bored about ⅛ inch closer to the shoulder from the mark. This ⅛ inch

◀ *These identification marks are on a structure in New Orleans.*

is not measured, just eyeballed. If it is a little more or a little less, the amount the peg is driven can compensate. Pegs are driven until they sound right.

Identification Marks

With Scribe Rule framing, you must mark all the components for reassembly; each piece has a number or mark corresponding to the adjacent timber. In Square Rule framing, though, every piece need not be marked as there are many interchangeable pieces (floor joists, braces, and rafters), and many old Square Rule frames were not marked at all. These marks can be Roman numerals cut with a chisel, a race knife (timber scribe), or ink, crayon, or pencil marks. I will describe a traditional marking system. The bents or crossframes are numbered *I, II, III,* and *IIII* starting from the west. In old frames, the Roman numeral *IV* was not used for *four* as it was too easy to confuse it with *six (VI)*. Likewise, *VIIII* was used

▲ *Lathe-turned pegs were used in this late nineteenth- or early twentieth-century barn in Windsor, Massachusetts.*

LAYING OUT AND CUTTING TIMBERS

▲ *This girding beam has three 1½-inch chisel marks. It is located in the third bent on the north end and its reference face is up.*

for *nine* instead of *IX*. Sometimes the *nine* was a *V* with a *I* inside. I mark the timbers on the north wall with a 1½-inch chisel and the timbers on the south with 2-inch chisel marks. A timber that spans from the north wall to the south wall, such as a girding beam, will have the same number at each end, but the numbers will have different sizes. Numbers are always on the primary reference face and are cut across the grain. Use two chisel cuts to create a V-shaped incised number. Thus, with only four numbers and two chisel sizes, the entire house frame can be labeled.

Stacking Finished Timbers

When finished with a timber, stack it in an orderly pile that allows air to circulate. Stack the parts in numerical order with identification numbers facing up. If like members are all stacked side by side and the ends lined up, mistakes in length are easily spotted. Check off timbers on the drawings as they are finished.

CHAPTER SIX

Building on the Frame

The Foundation

The foundation for the project house need not be substantially different from a conventional house foundation, and a 10- or 12-inch thick concrete wall is fine. It can be a poured, reinforced concrete foundation or it can be laid up with concrete blocks. You also have a choice of either a full basement or a crawl space with a frost wall and insulated flooring and plumbing (I recommend against using a pier foundation except for unheated buildings). I prefer a full basement for routing utilities, a root cellar, and to ensure that the first floor won't be exposed to winter winds from below—see Huff (1976) for more information. If you have the masonry skills, time, and desire—and the local building codes permit—you could even build a traditional stone foundation. However, in lieu of a full stone wall, you may choose to add a 4-inch wide shelf in the wall above grade to support a stone facing to cover the concrete and give the house a more

▲ *Our project house foundation has a shelf for a stone facing that measures 4 inches wide and 16 inches high.*

▲ *This reconstructed ell is built on a foundation of coursed rubble.*

solid, traditional appearance. The stone foundation walls of more expensive old houses were often faced above grade with brick or sawn stone slabs approximately 4 inches thick and several feet long. Investigate the older houses in your area to determine your regional vernacular. The outside dimension of the foundation must be at least 2 inches larger on all sides than the frame, so add 4 inches to the frame size, which gives exterior dimensions of 18 feet 4 inches by 36 feet 4 inches. If you go with a 12-inch thick wall, add 6 inches to the frame size.

Under all the interior basement posts, place a concrete or stone footing to spread out the load on the soil. This footing should be sized to be adequate for your particular soil capacity. A 3-foot square 12-inch thick footing is usually enough. If the posts will rest on ledge, only a column base of concrete or stone is necessary to keep the post bottom a few inches off the floor and prevent water from wicking up the post from the floor slab.

The frame needs to be anchored to the foundation. In the past, the timber sills merely sat on the stonework. The weight of the house pressing down on continuous sills tied the top of the stonework together. There weren't any anchors to keep the house from lifting up or blowing off. The substantial weight prevented uplift in all but the fiercest hurricane, tornado, or earthquake. If a house did lift off under such conditions, it might still be intact and able to be put back on the foundation. Had it been rigidly attached as with today's homes, it would have been destroyed rather than moved. One has to wonder which approach is better! Sill anchors prevent the foundation walls from buckling in under pressure from the earth, which is obviously important; the top of the wall relies upon the floor frame to resist these forces.

There are two effective ways to attach our house to the foundation. The way that is most familiar and appealing to conventional carpenters is to anchor a 2x10 mudsill with anchor bolts. The mudsill lies flush with the timber sills so that the wall planking can be nailed to it at the bottom. Although the timbers of the frame are not anchored directly, the planking should hold the frame to the sill. Another and perhaps easier way is to use flexible steel straps embedded in the wall that can be nailed to the sill timbers. These straps can be bent to conform to the sills and can even wrap around them. Because all the vertical wall planks are nailed to the sills, the house cannot move. The width, gauge, and length of these straps must be sufficient to meet the codes in your area. Check with your code official.

Most codes require that wood touching the foundation be an approved, rot-resistant variety. Although most new houses use pressure-treated lumber, it is environmentally better to use a local, naturally rot-resistant species such as

BUILD A CLASSIC TIMBER-FRAMED HOUSE

white oak, black locust, black cherry, or cedar. Most of the old timber-framed buildings that I have studied, however, used the same species for sills as for the rest of the frame. Although many old sills have rotted, many also survive that are not of rot-resistant species. I believe that a stone foundation does not draw up as much water to the sills as concrete, so the sills stay drier.

It is easiest to install the floor framing if the foundation is backfilled first. Bear in mind, however, that a concrete wall doesn't reach its full strength for nearly a month and cannot take a lot of soil pressure; backfill with care. Because concrete is a good conductor of heat, it is probably wise to insulate the wall, and rigid insulation is often applied against the foundation wall before it is backfilled to prevent heat loss. However, consider insulating on the inside rather than the outside. When installed on the exterior, rigid insulation needs some protection where it is exposed above grade, whether covered with stucco or some form of cement board. The insulation won't be durable like the concrete wall itself and can form a great hideaway for carpenter ants.

Assembling the Framing

Before the actual raising, the sill timbers and first-floor joists should be set, leveled, and squared. The most convenient way to set the sills is to put them up on blocks from 2 to 4 inches high. This allows you to drive the pins from the top (reference face) and saw them off below. It also allows clearance for planks to roll or slide the sills up if the foundation is not backfilled. Use rot-resistant species for the pegs into the sills. Assemble one of the long sills first on the wall, plug the cross

sills into it, and then put pegs loosely in the joints. The two sill girders will need temporary support at their free ends. Forget the basement posts for now. Starting in the middle bay, insert only the tenoned joists into their mortises. You can spread the free end of the cross sills to accomplish this. Put pegs in these holes loosely. Insert the end sills and their tying joists. Assemble the other long sill next to its position on blocks or planks, and then slide it onto the four cross sill tenons, starting at one end of the sill. Insert and drive all pegs until joints are tight and the pegs are resisting. Square up the assembly and at the same time position it equidistant from the outside of the foundation wall on all four sides. Make sure the long walls with the scarfs are straight, too. The assembly can be levered into position with a long pry bar or tapped with a heavy commander (a large wooden mallet). Check for squareness by measuring the frame's diagonals; when the frame is square, the diagonals will be equal. Nail

A. BLAKE GARDNER

◀ *Timbers can be rolled on the wall using pipe rollers.*

a long diagonal (a 20-foot long 2x6 is good) on the top of the assembly to keep it square until the sills are lowered onto the foundation wall.

Starting at one end, pry up and remove the blocks, being careful not to move the assembly sideways. If you are using 4-inch high or higher blocks, lower the frame first onto 2-inch blocks all around before repeating the procedure to lower the frame onto the foundation. Now the top surface of the sills must be leveled. Using a transit or water level, find any high spots (don't worry about the two sill girders yet). All of the assembly must be shimmed up with cedar shingles to the elevation of the highest spot, and place the shims at post locations, under scarfs, and in the middle of end walls. If there is a crown in these end wall sills, allow enough space for them to settle straight when the floor weight is applied. Fiberglass batt insulation can be stuffed under these sills later. Check the diagonals again for squareness and look over overall positioning and adjust if necessary. Bend the sill anchors up (if appropriate) and nail them into the sides of the sills.

The basement posts go in now. You want the post bottom off the finished basement slab by at least a couple of inches to prevent moisture wicking. The simplest support is a squarish stone, at least 6 inches high, on the footing under the post that is wedged up tight to the post bottom until the sill girder is level. Later, when the slab is poured around it, the stone will be anchored in place. With the weight of the house on it, the post bottom will conform to the irregular surface of the stone and be unmovable. If you live in earthquake- or hurricane-prone areas, you might use an anchor strap here also.

The remainder of the floor joists can now be inserted into their pockets. Start both ends in at the same time. You now need some sort of temporary floor to work on. You could apply the subfloor now, but if it is dry, seasoned material you are taking a chance. A good soaking rain can cause subflooring to heave and buckle. I

▲ *Walk the center sill girders across the basement on a scaffolding of sawhorses. The free end needs temporary support until the other longitudinal sill is in place.*

▶*Make minor adjustments to the sill framing using the commander.*

BUILD A CLASSIC TIMBER-FRAMED HOUSE

prefer to use loose boards or planks as a temporary floor. After the roof and walls are on, a good subfloor can be installed without risk. If you use 1-inch thick boards, use a double layer for extra strength during the raising. The future roof and attic floorboards or wall planking could be used. Be sure the openings in the floor have good solid coverage.

If the house site is muddy, pick up some hay bales from a local farmer and spread the hay around the foundation and work area. Hay does wonders in keeping muddy footprints off your house frame.

Assembling the Bents

I like to have as much of the frame preassembled before the raising as possible. Preassembly makes the house raising go faster and that keeps everyone interested. The four bents or crossframes can be assembled on the deck in reverse order of their raising. The last bent to go up is assembled first. Because the bents are taller than the space between them, they cannot all be preassembled on the deck with post tenons next to their respective mortises. If the site permits, it may be easiest to assemble the two end bents on blocks or sawhorses on the adjacent ground. Since the reference face would be down, the pegs should be driven from below. If the land slopes off too much, raising bents this way isn't feasible. In the photos of the house raising, the height of the deck off-grade made it necessary to assemble all bents on the deck. Two of the bents had to be moved along the deck as they were raised.

When assembling bents, first put the girding beam up on blocks, which allows pegs to be driven through and keeps the bents cleaner. Then put braces into the girding beam and slide the posts on their

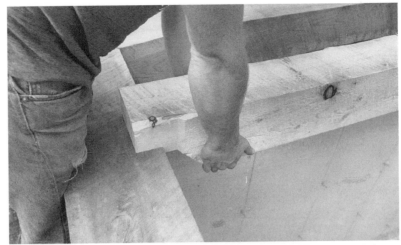

▲ *Once the sills are squared and leveled, the remainder of the joists can be inserted.*

▲ *The floor frame is complete.*

▲ *Install a temporary floor to provide a footing during the raising.*

▲ *The bents are assembled and ready for the raising.*

tenons. Peg all connections. Drive pegs from the reference side until they are tight. They can be driven more later so don't saw the ends off. Position the post bottom tenons next to their respective mortises where possible.

Organize the remainder of the timbers so they are readily available when needed. Identification numbers should be up. For raising day, you need a pair of heavy pry bars, six sawhorses, staging planks (at least six 2x10s that are 8 to 12 feet long), two 2x6s at least 10 feet long, two 50-foot lengths of ½-inch manila rope, a commander, and possibly a come-along if joints are going together tightly. You can make your own commander from timber cut-offs (lots of knots are fine) and a tapered replacement shovel handle. Drill a hole through the head — usually about 1½ inches wide — and insert the thinnest end of the handle first. The thick end will wedge itself in the head and tighten with use, much like the handle of a pick ax.

I usually schedule a raising for a Saturday with the following Sunday as a rain date. As soon as enough helpers arrive, the raising begins and moves quickly. Before lifting the first bent, a short speech on safety is imperative. You don't want this momentous occasion to be marred by an accident or injury. One person must take command and orchestrate the raising, and others must listen for this person's directions. Individual responsibilities should be given to specific individuals. Dogs, children, and others not directly involved should be well back from the work area. Remove any clutter from the deck. Have a first aid kit handy and know where the nearest phone is in case of emergencies. Don't forget to not serve alcoholic beverages until the raising is over. Finally, you may wish to invite any experienced framers in your area to lend their raising expertise.

On top of the two tall posts, loop a rope to use as a tag line to keep the bents from going over. One person should be positioned at the foot of each post to help hold the post bottoms and to guide the tenons into their respective mortises. Those at the main posts should have a long (at least 4 feet) pry bar in the mortise to keep the post from sliding. Those

A. BLAKE GARDNER

▶ *The post bottom is guided into its mortise; a long bar prevents the bent from sliding off the deck.*

lifting the bent should be lifting straight up and walking forward as they do but there is invariably a tendency to push the bent horizontally as well. The person using the pry bar resists this force. It would be disastrous if the end bent was to slide off the deck as it was lifted. The pry bars also guide the tenon into the mortise but the bar is withdrawn before it becomes pinched in the joint. Occasionally the post tenons do not engage as the bent is lifted, but as long as the posts are not off the deck, the bent should be raised vertically. With a few taps of the commander, you can align the tenons with their mortises and the post will drop 2 inches with a resounding thud. Start at one end and work toward the other, keeping toes and fingers out from underneath posts. Working one end at a time, plumb the post on the reference face with a 4-foot level and securely nail at a minimum a 10-foot 2x6 diagonal brace from the post down to the deck at about a 45-degree angle. Avoid covering any joints or peg holes. These braces should be left on until the plates with their braces are on.

The second bent follows. When it is vertical, the tying joist and the two girts with their braces need to be inserted. Set up a pair of sawhorses with planks across them under each of the members. Then three or four helpers standing on the planks can insert the members. When all are engaged, push the bents together—assisting with the commander as necessary—and peg all connections. The other joists can be dropped in at this time.

Continue with the other two bents until the second-floor framing is complete. The second floor should be covered with loosely laid planks or two layers of boards. The future wall planks are fine for this. Leave a sufficient hole in the middle

◀ *Each post is plumbed and a temporary diagonal brace is nailed on to secure it.*

▲ *The second bent is raised. Note the two pike poles.*

▶ *The girts with braces and the tying joists must be inserted between the bents. Planks set on sawhorses make convenient staging.*

▶ *All the remaining floor joists are fitted.*

of the floor to pass up long timbers. The plates are next. Set up a continuous scaffold on sawhorses along the front posts. The plate sections are first carried onto the first-floor deck, then passed up through to the second-floor deck and set on the staging on blocks. The plate section with the lower half of the scarf is, of course, put on first. The bridled scarf was chosen to allow the plate sections to be inserted separately. With some other scarfs, such as a bladed scarf, the plate would be assembled first and then lowered on the posts. With as many hands as room allows, lift the plate onto the posts and engage each tenon as it is lowered. Should the posts have bows, a smaller bar can be used to align the joints or try a

▲ *A temporary flooring of planks is laid to make work above the second floor easier.*

▲ *In preparation for raising the plates, braces are installed and pegged to hold them in position.*

▼ *The plates are passed up through the floor.*

▲ *Each plate is lifted onto post and brace tenons. Planks over sawhorses are again used for staging.*

▶ *The tie beams follow the plates. The commander can be used to seat them.*

couple taps with the commander. Repeat for the other plate half and then set up your equipment again and do the opposite side's plate. Peg all these joints.

The attic level framing is next. Set up the sawhorses and planks to provide a staging to lift each tie beam starting with end tie beam 1. The plates may have to be spread or pulled together to align the dovetailed lap joint. Keep moving the staging east and insert the attic floor joists as you go. The chimney opening framing is easily installed by spreading the joists. I suggest that you add a few 20d (or "20 penny") spikes to keep these joints tight. For convenience, put on the last tie beam before the last three joists. It can be set on the plates and can slide along until it drops into its dovetail.

With the attic framing complete, boards can be laid to provide a working platform for the roof structure. First, insert the rafters with the tenoned bottoms and peg them, remembering that the mortised rafters are on the north side. The raising planks are cut to length and fitted between them. Align a straight, nonwaney edge so that it just touches the top plane of the rafters and spike it to each joist and the tie beams with two 20d (4-inch) common nails. Once the raising plates are fastened, all the rafters can be added. The common rafters are centered above every other attic floor joist and each one is spiked to the raising plate with three 20d common nails. The center opening between the rafters must be 32 inches wide to allow for the chimney. To achieve the straightest roof plane, stretch a string across the truss rafters near their lower end and slide the common rafters until they just touch this string. Check to see if the peaks are also in line. When all rafters are up, they need to be plumbed and spaced properly. Plumb the first rafter with a long level or plumb bob and nail a board brace on its top side to the lower end of another rafter at about a 45-degree angle. Then, measure from the outside of the building to each rafter's reference side at its foot and make the distance the same at the peak. Nail a board parallel with the ridge across the rafters to secure the spacing. Add another opposing diagonal brace at the opposite end. These braces and spacing boards stiffen the roof until the board sheathing is applied. Once one side is sheathed, the braces are removed and the other side is sheathed. Nail a small evergreen tree to the peak at one end to give thanks to the forest for providing such a wonderful, useful material as wood, and let the celebration begin.

Pike Poles. When tall barn frames were raised in the past, helpers would use pike poles, which are 2- to 3-inch diameter poles up to 16 feet long with a spiked point. As the bent was raised and passed from reach, those with pikes jabbed them into the upper timbers to help push the bent up. Our house frame can be raised without pikes because the bents are not out of reach. If you have pikes available, it would be helpful to have one on each of the tall posts. Those holding the pikes

▲ *Work from one end of the building to the other when installing the joists and tie beams.*

A.BLAKE GARDNER

▶ *The principal rafters are inserted first and pegged. The raising plates are then cut to fit and securely fastened. Common rafters are then nailed to the raising plate. Allow enough clearance between the central rafter pairs for the chimney.*

A.BLAKE GARDNER

▶ *After attaching the traditional evergreen bough to the peak, helpers pose for a picture on the finished house frame.*

BUILD A CLASSIC TIMBER-FRAMED HOUSE

should have enough control so that if the bent jerked and a pike dropped down, the pike can be kept from hitting someone below.

Using a Gin Pole. This house can be raised safely without the benefit of a big crew in a manner that is as old as the art of building itself. The gin pole (*gin* is the root of *engine*) is a simple but ingenious method of lifting loads vertically. You need a strong, straight, relatively knot-free pole about 10 feet longer than the highest lift. On our frame, a 32-foot pole should do. The tip should be at least 5 inches in diameter and the butt perhaps 8 inches. The pole is guyed nearly vertical by three guy lines anchored to immovable objects. The top of the pole should lean so it lies almost directly above the object to be lifted. I say *almost* because the guy lines will stretch some and cause the pole to lean more as the object is raised. Two guy lines should angle back to hold up the pole while the third acts as a stay to keep the pole from tipping over backward should the load swing toward it. At the top of the pole, leave a branch stub to keep the lines from slipping down the pole. If there is no stub, bore a hole and insert a peg with a 1-inch or larger diameter. The rope that the tackles are hung from is looped around the pole a few times above the branch stub. All lines that attach to the pole should be looped around the pole in such a manner that they tighten as the load is applied. The butt of the pole can sit in a shallow hole in the ground or can rest on the floor decking. If the pole rests on the deck, be sure there is adequate support below and enough anchorage to the deck to keep the pole from sliding, although most of the force is straight down.

The block and tackle provides the mechanical advantage necessary for limited muscle power to lift heavy loads. The more pulleys in each block, the easier the lift will be. For instance, using two double-pulley blocks with one block having a shackle to attach the end of the rope to gives you nearly a 4-to-1 advantage (some energy is lost to friction). With two triple-pulley blocks, you have nearly a 6-to-1 advantage. Of course, the more pulleys

▲ *The gin pole is a marvelous device for lifting heavy objects safely and without strain. This 30-foot long spruce gin pole allowed only three men to raise this cruck frame.*

involved, the longer the rope must be. To determine the mechanical advantage of the setup, count the number of lines supporting the lower block. Five lines means about a 5-to-1 ratio. The line coming out of the upper block that you pull on should be passed through another pulley anchored at the base of the gin pole. This pulley doesn't change the mechanical advantage, only the direction of the pull. On a downward pull, two or maybe three people can effectively pull. With a horizontal pull, numerous people can pull in line.

The main drawback to the gin pole is that it has to be moved for each lift. Because of this and the extra setup time, I only use a gin pole if a hand raising won't work, such as when lifting trusses or very tall bents.

After the Frame

The Roof

As soon as the frame is topped off, tackle the roof. Completing the roof pro-

tects the frame from rain and from drying too quickly, keeps water out of the basement, and gives you a dry place to work in the rain. One of the advantages of having an unheated attic below the roof is that the house can be roofed more quickly and with less expense than insulating on top of a timber-framed roof.

I suggest a roof sheathing of 1-inch rough-sawn boards. They can be waney, green, low-grade boards of virtually any species. They can even be random widths and lengths. They should, however, be at least 6 inches wide and 8 inches is better. Start on the side of the roof without the temporary bracing and lay them as tightly as you can without being fussy. If the boards are laid green, gaps will widen as they dry and shrink. The gaps are good for ventilation. Allow the proper overhangs on both the eaves and gable ends. To avoid setting up a scaffold to board the roof, work from the inside. The chimney opening allows even the last boards to be installed that way. For the roof, sawn wood shingles are recommended.

If you must buy your shingles, western red cedar is the best choice. Use 18-inch shingles with 5½ inches to the weather, which is triple coverage. However, they can also be sawn from your own trees with little impact on the environment. The traditional choice in much of New England is eastern white pine. These pines grow with a whorl of branches added each year, and healthy trees grow between 6 inches and 4 feet in height annually. You want to cut your shingles in the clear wood between these whorls. If you are selecting trees for shingles, pick larger specimens with whorls spaced about 2 feet apart. Since most shingle sawmills need squared balks to work with, first saw logs into the largest timber that has mostly heartwood. Then saw the logs in half right through the pith, which provides mostly radially sawn shingles, and radially sawn shingles are less likely to warp. Next, measure out 18-inch clear wood billets between the whorls. If some whorls are less than 18 inches apart, saw the billets at 18 inches anyway and keep the knots at one end. These billets will still provide some usable shingles.

The Wall Sheathing

Traditional wall sheathing for a plank house is full-height planks that are 12 to 20 inches wide and at least 1¼ inches thick or, more often, 1½ inches thick. In my area, spruce, hemlock, and pine were the common choices. They were rough-sawn and probably unseasoned. Because of their great width, the nails wouldn't let them cup. They might split, but that would hardly affect their performance. Today, full-height planks of such width

are hard to procure and expensive. You could use wide planks that are only one story in height or 2x6 or 2x8 tongue-and-groove planks, which can be milled locally or purchased from the lumber yard. If you purchase the planks from the lumber-yard, use a commercial grade for economy—the planking will not be seen anyway. The tongue-and-groove joints keep the planks acting as a unit.

Windows and Doors

After the planks are up, you can mark your rough window and door openings using a level. Locate rough openings the proper distance off your floor so that the finish height inside the jamb is 6 feet 8 inches. Rough openings are usually 6 feet 10½ inches off the subfloor. The fenestration (window and door arrangement) seen in the photos and drawings is very traditional, but you may opt for something more contemporary. Keep the corners of

◄ *The wall planking can be installed with or without first framing window and door openings. You will save lumber, however, if you frame them initially.*

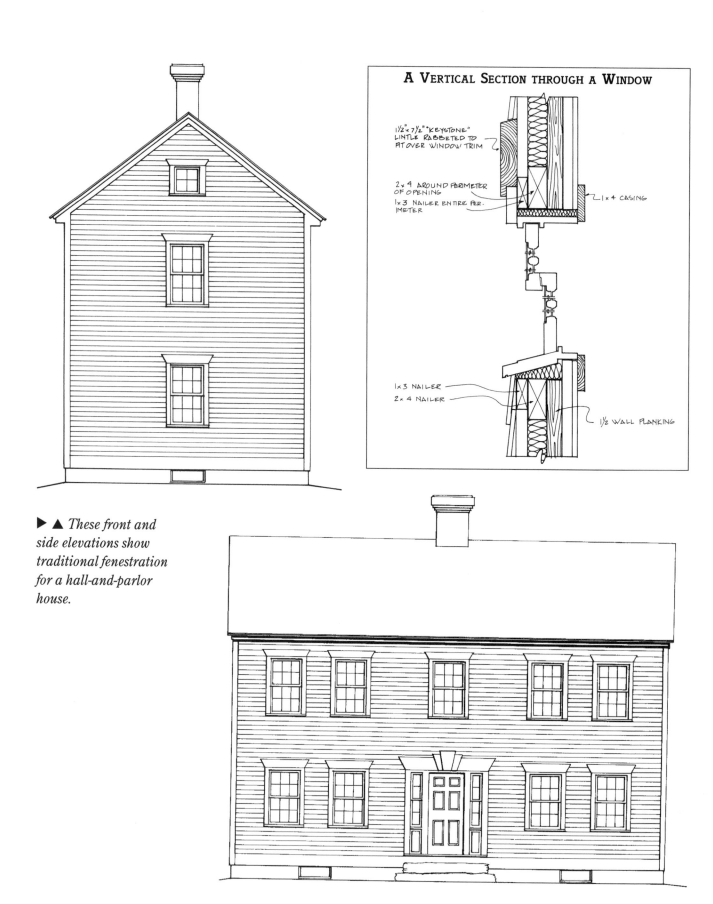

A VERTICAL SECTION THROUGH A WINDOW

1½" × 7½" "KEYSTONE" LINTLE RABBETED TO FIT OVER WINDOW TRIM

2 × 4 AROUND PERIMETER OF OPENING

1 × 3 NAILER ENTIRE PERIMETER

1 × 4 CASING

1 × 3 NAILER

2 × 4 NAILER

1½ WALL PLANKING

▶ ▲ *These front and side elevations show traditional fenestration for a hall-and-parlor house.*

the windows tight to the braces. To stiffen an opening and provide nailing on the outside for the furring strips, nail a flat, full-sized (rough-sawn) 2x4 around the exterior of the opening.

You can build your own plank door with battens. Use a rot-resistant species for the sill, frame, and door. You could install a used door if you like. Plan your rough opening appropriately. Some old houses had very extravagant entries, and if you have woodworking skills you might want to try one. If you choose a new door, choose a solid-wood one. Solid wood wears more gracefully than metal or plastic. Add a storm door (with divided lights, of course) to protect the door.

Wall Insulation

Over the wall planks we must install a vapor barrier or retarder because the

▲ *Simple and strong plank doors are often the most economical entryway choice.*

▲ *These fancy entrances are found at Old Deerfield, Massachusetts.*

building codes require it. I'm not sure if we really do need one—warm, cozy buildings have been built without them for thousands of years. There is also some debate on how long they actually last inside the wall. Are they permanent enough for as permanent a dwelling as ours? These sorts of products are constantly changing, so do your homework before deciding on one.

Over the vapor barrier, put your rigid insulation. The furring strips that the siding is nailed to hold the insulation in place. The practical thickness for the insulation is 2 inches as the nails holding the furring strips must penetrate it. I use 16d box nails. If you must use more insulation, add some nailers—2x3s on edge

(if rough-sawn) would allow 3 inches of insulation. The insulation used in our project house was rigid fiberglass. It wasn't chosen because it is highly efficient (its R-value is 8.7 for a 2-inch thickness) or because it is cost-effective. Rigid fiberglass breathes, doesn't use CFCs, isn't prone to attack by carpenter ants, and isn't made from fossil fuels. Carefully consider your choices of insulation—it may be one of the more important building material decisions that you make. You must weigh such factors as efficiency, durability, economics, and environmental friendliness. By the time this book is printed, there may be some new (or old) insulation solutions developed that answer all the criteria superbly.

A Wall Section at the Cornice

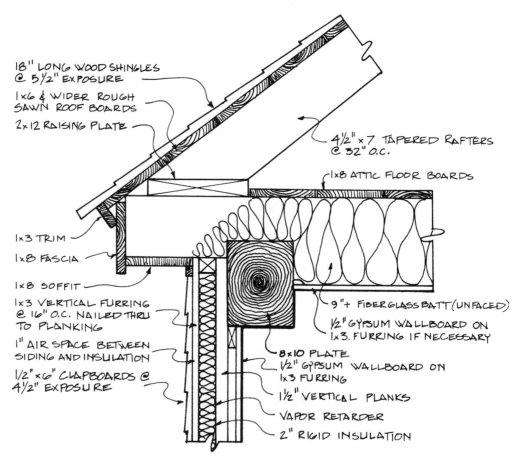

18" LONG WOOD SHINGLES @ 5½" EXPOSURE

1x6 & WIDER ROUGH SAWN ROOF BOARDS

2x12 RAISING PLATE

4½" x 7 TAPERED RAFTERS @ 32" O.C.

1x8 ATTIC FLOOR BOARDS

1x3 TRIM

1x8 FASCIA

1x8 SOFFIT

1x3 VERTICAL FURRING @ 16" O.C. NAILED THRU TO PLANKING

1" AIR SPACE BETWEEN SIDING AND INSULATION

½" x 6" CLAPBOARDS @ 4½" EXPOSURE

9"+ FIBERGLASS BATT (UNFACED)

½" GYPSUM WALLBOARD ON 1x3 FURRING IF NECESSARY

8x10 PLATE

½" GYPSUM WALLBOARD ON 1x3 FURRING

1½" VERTICAL PLANKS

VAPOR RETARDER

2" RIGID INSULATION

BUILD A CLASSIC TIMBER-FRAMED HOUSE

Plank Walls without Insulation

There is an alternative to insulated walls. First, you could build the house without the vapor barrier, furring, and insulation. With lath and plaster on the inside to keep out drafts, a 1½-inch plank wall with clapboards will have an R-value of less than 5. If you don't keep the house above 60 degrees in the winter and if you burn your own wood for fuel, you can probably get by. Many older plank houses had thicker planks—up to 4 inches thick—which gave an R-value of about 8. That's still not great, but the walls do begin to function more like a log house, becoming a heat reservoir that stores the sun's heat during the day and slowly releases it at night. A massive plank wall performs better than its R-value might suggest. For ease of handling, I propose using two layers of planks with the joints staggered.

Siding

There are several options for the siding: shingles, clapboards, vertical shiplap boards, board and batten, diagonal boards, and even stucco. The exterior finish you choose should be based on those materials available in your locale and what is or was common there historically. If you are building on Cape Cod, for instance, white cedar shingles are probably the most appropriate. In the hill towns of western Massachusetts where I live and work, native red spruce or white pine clapboards are the traditional choice. A few houses from the 1700s still have the original clapboards fastened with wrought nails, and some haven't seen a coat of paint for at least one hundred years. These aren't the clapboards that we find at the lumberyard today—they were not

A WALL SECTION AT THE FOUNDATION

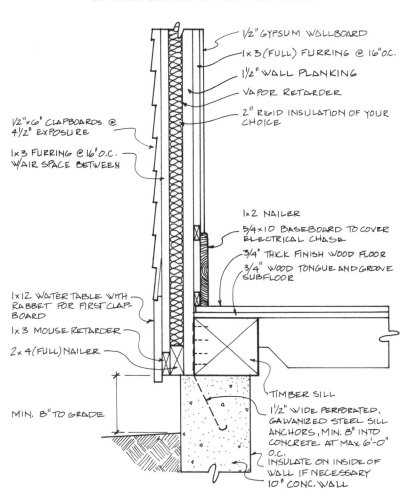

- ½" GYPSUM WALLBOARD
- 1x3 (FULL) FURRING @ 16" O.C.
- 1½" WALL PLANKING
- VAPOR RETARDER
- 2" RIGID INSULATION OF YOUR CHOICE
- ½"x6" CLAPBOARDS @ 4½" EXPOSURE
- 1x3 FURRING @ 16" O.C. W/ AIR SPACE BETWEEN
- 1x2 NAILER
- 5/4x10 BASEBOARD TO COVER ELECTRICAL CHASE
- 3/4" THICK FINISH WOOD FLOOR
- 3/4" WOOD TONGUE AND GROOVE SUBFLOOR
- 1x12 WATER TABLE WITH RABBET FOR FIRST CLAPBOARD
- 1x3 MOUSE RETARDER
- 2x4 (FULL) NAILER
- MIN. 8" TO GRADE
- TIMBER SILL
- 1½" WIDE PERFORATED, GALVANIZED STEEL SILL ANCHORS, MIN. 8" INTO CONCRETE AT MAX. 6'-0" O.C.
- INSULATE ON INSIDE OF WALL IF NECESSARY
- 10" CONC. WALL

A SECTION THROUGH THE RAKE

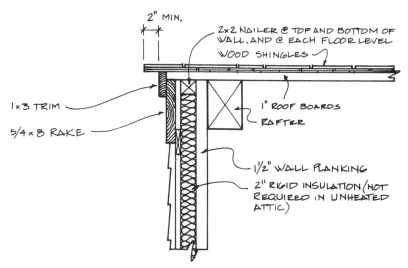

- 2" MIN.
- 2x2 NAILER @ TOP AND BOTTOM OF WALL, AND @ EACH FLOOR LEVEL
- WOOD SHINGLES
- 1x3 TRIM
- 5/4 x 8 RAKE
- 1" ROOF BOARDS
- RAFTER
- 1½" WALL PLANKING
- 2" RIGID INSULATION (NOT REQUIRED IN UNHEATED ATTIC)

sawn with a taper. A common size was a rough-sawn ½x6. Occasionally, opposite corners might be tapered back a few inches with a plane to lay flatter. Because they were cut from the primeval forests where trees grew slowly, there was little

▲ *Traditionally, clapboards were scarfed at their ends where they join.*

▶ *This scarf was cut with the adz in about 15 seconds while the jig held it in place. One foot is placed on the clapboard to keep it from sliding.*

if any sapwood on them, and heartwood will not rot if given adequate light and ventilation. Instead, these old-style clapboards wore away gradually and produced those wonderful furrows and colors that we treasure.

Installing Clapboards. Clapboards are nailed over vertical furring strips every 16 inches on center. Nailers are also provided around windows and doors or wherever the ends need support. At the bottom of the wall, a wide board called a *water table* could be installed and the first clapboard fitted over it, although in the house photographed here the owner didn't use one. If you omit the water table, install a continuous strip of wood to cant out the first clapboard. This strip or the water table also serves to keep mice and bats from inhabiting the air space behind the siding. Six-inch clapboards are typically exposed 4½ inches, but this can be changed slightly to end up with a whole clapboard below a window instead of one nearly cut through.

Today, carpenters merely butt clapboards at their ends and waterproof the joint with a piece of asphalt-coated paper below. On houses from the eighteenth and early nineteenth centuries in my area, clapboards were adzed to create a scarf where they join. The scarf was typically 2 inches long, which is the width of the blade of the framing square. In this way, the clapboards truly shed the water. This scarfing sounds like a painstaking detail but it actually goes quite quickly. On the spruce clapboards for my workshop, each end was adzed in about fifteen seconds. Be sure that you locate the scarf in clear grain. One reason why today's carpenters use the square butt joint is that a scarf of the type described is not easy to cut with

When I was planning my house some years ago, I fully intended to live there without electric power. I thought that if I did eventually want power, it would be produced on-site. I have softened a bit over the years and the house is completely wired and connected to the grid, but I am not a big user of the stuff. In addition to the lights, water heater, and pump, I have backup electric heat to keep my pipes from freezing when I leave town in winter for a few days. Because I hadn't planned on getting electrical service, the meter and drop ended up being right next to my front door. Although I don't like the looks of it, at least I take notice of how much power I am using when I pass it.

Before you automatically install your electric service, give it some consideration. Do a little research into the effects of electromagnetic fields on health. Decide if you really need and want power. If you do, maybe it can be produced on-site (from wind, solar panels, water). By making intelligent siting choices and a few life-style changes, you can eliminate many of the items that require power. If there is a water source uphill of the house, a gravity-fed water system can replace the water pump. If you can your produce and have a cold cellar, you won't need a refrigerator/ freezer. If sited to take advantage of solar heat gain, you can heat your house and hot water with the sun. If you do all you can to replace electric-powered devices but you still need electricity, at least you won't be using as much. The smaller the load, the easier it will be to produce it on-site.

If you tie into the grid, use the smallest amperage service that you can. As the cost of electricity skyrockets, it's likely our need for it will diminish rather than increase. Finally, don't repeat my mistake—plan where the service will come in!

Wiring a timber-framed house is a bit different than a conventional one. For each different exterior-wall enclosure system, there is at least one different preferred wiring system. For our plank-walled house, exterior walls have the wiring on the inside to keep the wiring from piercing the insulation/vapor barrier envelope. The easiest system provides an electrical chase behind a baseboard or wainscoting. Since the interior walls are conventional 2x4 stud-framed walls, try to locate most of the wiring there. If possible, put wall switches and wall-mounted lights there. Use surface-mounted wiring (Wiremold) for fixtures on exterior walls. If used sparingly, it is unobtrusive.

◀ *In this house, the wiring in the kitchen/ dining area will be covered by wainscoting. In the rest of the house, the wiring runs behind a baseboard. The 1-inch furring strips that span the planks can support wallboard.*

▲ *If you locate the clapboard scarf in a clear section of wood, your work will be easier.*

▲ *Accordion lath was made from thin boards that were split and stretched out over a wall. The riven edges provided good keying for plaster.*

power tools, a problem compounded by the tapered clapboards common today.

Interior Wall Finish

In traditional plank houses, lath and plaster were applied over the interior of the planks. Lath was made up of wide boards approximately ½-inch thick that often spanned the length of the room. Originally, lath was riven and expanded to cover the wall. Because of the way in which the laths were riven, it was called *accordion lath*. The riven edges formed great keys for holding plaster. This horizontal lath nailed across the planks stiffened the wall, as did the clapboards on the opposite side. Thus, the wall plane acted as a unit rather than as lots of individual planks, forming an eighteenth-century version of plywood sheathing. Builders applied a three-coat plaster finish made from lime, sand, and hair over the lath. Later, gypsum plaster became standard. Lath and plaster were a wonderful system. The lath was sawn from local timber, the plaster was often produced locally, and area craftsmen did the work. This lath-and-plaster system can certainly be used on your house. It is, of course, labor intensive compared to gypsum wallboard, and plastering is perhaps best accomplished by professionals. However, should you choose to do it yourself, you need not achieve a perfectly flat surface. The resulting textured wall is actually more appropriate to a timber frame. However, most will probably opt for gypsum wallboard as it is indeed faster. For wallboard, run horizontal 1x3 furring strips every 16 inches on center over the planks and around all edges and at timbers. In lieu of the traditional lath, furring strips will stiffen the planks. The finish wall will extend out 1½ inches, concealing some

BUILD A CLASSIC TIMBER-FRAMED HOUSE

of the timber framing. Some concealment is actually more authentic looking for old-style houses. Where the wallboard butts the timbers, you can either run taping compound right up to the timbers or tape to ½-inch L-bead. The L-bead is a metal strip nailed over the wallboard, much like corner bead, that is taped over and concealed, making a clean, straight edge when the timber shrinks away from the wallboard. Leave off the wallboard at the base of the wall for the baseboard electrical chase.

Interior Partitions

For the interior partitions of our house, conventional 2x4 stud walls were used to facilitate wiring and plumbing and gypsum wallboard covered both sides. In old plank-on-timber frame houses, interior partitions were composed of wide planks nailed to the sides of floor and ceiling timbers. These were lathed and plastered on both sides creating a wall about 3 inches thick. The disadvantage of this old system is that there is no cavity to conceal pipes and wires. Since the timber frame is designed to carry the floor loads, these interior partitions are not load-bearing.

Finishing and Insulating the Second-Floor Ceiling

If the attic floor joists are rough sawn, they will likely vary in depth. If you install a traditional lath-and-plaster ceiling, you probably won't have to do any shimming. If you use gypsum wallboard, however, you may wish to furr the ceiling with 1x3s shimmed level. Although wallboard over furring lowers the ceiling a little, it provides more space for insulation. If the joists are consistent in size, furring may not be necessary.

Some building codes allow you to omit the vapor barrier in the ceiling if the attic is ventilated. If we use board decking with wood shingles, the whole roof surface allows air movement. I would opt to omit the vapor barrier here if your codes permit it so that the house will breathe, vent any toxic vapors, and decrease the interior humidity level.

For ceiling insulation, I suggest either loose-fill or batt-type insulation. Mineral wool batts (fiberglass), cellulose, mica pellets (vermiculite), or even something of your own concoction might be appropriate. Your choice depends on local availability, cost, health risks, thermal performance, and building code requirements.

Floors

Because of the floor-joist spacing (every 30 inches on center), you must either use two layers of boards or a single plank with tongue-and-grooved edges that is at least 1½ inches thick if softwood or 1¼

▲ *The wallboard ceiling is fastened to 1x3s every 16 inches on center. Use shims if necessary.*

Like electricity, plumbing is one of those things we don't have to have. But doing without plumbing requires a bigger life-style change than electricity. If you have a composting toilet or outhouse and a hand pump in the kitchen, you can live as comfortably as you would have a century ago. You would have to heat the water and fill the bathtub by hand, but it would make bathing a ritual. In summer you could use a solar-heated outdoor shower or swim in a pond or stream. Before you rule these thoughts out, try staying at a country house without electricity or plumbing for a few weeks. A short time ago, it was seen as backward, but now some see it as progressive.

Because timber-framed homes predate the advent of indoor plumbing, they lack the cavities in the floor to hide such amenities. Fixtures on the first floor can have their plumbing ex-posed in the basement, but unless you want exposed plumbing in the ceiling of the first floor, you must plan carefully to conceal the pipes for second-floor fixtures. The simplest way is to locate all fixtures over a closet, pantry, bath, or other such space that can have a dropped ceiling. Then channel the piping down to the basement in a 2x6 stud partition. If all the plumbing fixtures are vertically in line, then a 2x6 partition can be located under them. If there is an open room below the bath, you could elevate the bathroom floor enough to run all the pipes above the second floor until they can drop down to the basement via the nearest partition. Of course, this requires a step up into the bathroom. In lieu of a raised bathroom floor, you could lower the second-floor timber framing in that bay about 6 inches so that the built-up floor will be flush with the rest of the second floor.

◀ *One option for hiding the plumbing in an upstairs bathroom is to raise the floor for a pipe chase. In that case, run 2x6 joists over the subfloor, which will force you to step up into the finished bathroom.*

inches thick if hardwood. In the well-to-do old houses, builders often installed wide hardwood planks (or yellow or hard pine) with tongue-and-grooved edges. The tongue-and-grooved edges stiffened the floor by spreading the load onto adjacent planks and also kept some of the dust from filtering through the floor. In common houses, a two-layer system without the tongue-and-groove was used. The joints were staggered to add strength and to keep the dirt from filtering through. The boards were face-nailed with wrought or cut nails.

In the areas that supported a northern hardwood forest, beech, yellow birch, and sugar maple were popular choices for the top boards. These species wear extremely well, and rooms seem brighter with their light coloring. Judging by the gaps between boards in some houses, they were laid down only partially seasoned. If you use hardwood flooring use cut-box nails (see Tremont Nail Company in Appendix B) so you won't have to pre-drill for each nail. A cut nail, if driven so the shaft is parallel with the grain, will not split hardwood like a wire nail. And, because the nails are visible, the heads on a cut nail are more attractive. The boards need not be clear. Indeed, buying all clear boards would be expensive. For my floor, I purchased rough-sawn mixed maple boards of random width that were "run of the mill" (that is, not sorted or graded). I stacked them to dry outside under cover for at least a year. When I got the roof on the frame, I stacked them inside on the subfloor. Then, just before I was ready to lay the floor, I had them planed on four sides at a local mill. They were ¾ inch thick and ranged from 3½ inches to 11¼ inches wide. Waney edges were placed down, and boards with unsound loose

▲ *This maple floor is made up of 1-inch thick random-width boards that were planed to ¾ inch after seasoning and face-nailed with cut-box nails. The floor is attractive, durable, and inexpensive.*

▲ *If you lay your floor over an unheated crawlspace, you can insulate between the nailers on top of the subfloor. The finish floor here is 2x6 tongue-and-groove planking.*

knots were avoided. The floor has a lot of character and I saved a great deal over the typical hardwood floors installed today. With wide boards, the joints between planks open and close depending on the seasonal humidity. Eventually, dirt and grime get packed in these joints and the floor looks like an eighteenth-century floor.

Some mills that plane boards can also tongue-and-groove edges. Then, if you use the thick stock sizes mentioned above, only one layer will be necessary.

For the second-story flooring, you can use the same system. The second floor's flooring is also the first-floor ceiling, so you may want to add some sound insulation to make the upstairs more private by installing ½-inch thick structural sound insulation board between the flooring layers. The insulation also helps to prevent dust from filtering through the ceiling. Many prefer softwood floors upstairs because softwoods are softer under shoeless feet and warmer to the touch, though they dent and scratch easier than hardwoods.

The attic floor was a place to use low-grade boards in the past and still is. Builders often laid the flooring quickly using rough-sawn boards with little regard for tight joints. If ever the attic becomes living space, just apply a finished layer of boards over the rough layer.

You will want to apply some sort of finish on your flooring to prevent staining. Though there are some very durable commercially manufactured finishes, I recommend using a natural finish. Many people that have been bombarded with chemicals for years have become sensitive to outgassing from these synthetic finishes. Sources for natural and low-odor synthetic finishes can be found in *The Healthy House* (Bower 1989).

When choosing finishes for any part of the house, try to select the healthiest, most environment-friendly products available. Remember that your house will last for many generations.

CHAPTER 7

Building Options

I chose the hall-and-parlor house for this book because its design is very flexible and easily modified. Because people's needs differ, you will probably want to customize the design to suit your requirements. You may want to start with a smaller structure and phase in the construction, or you may want a larger house — at the start or in time. This chapter presents some of your options.

Thinking Smaller

The Half House

Though the hall-and-parlor house is ideal as a starter home, some may wish to start out smaller. Smaller houses are becoming more popular as the cost of building rises, and some people just don't need much space. One option is to build a so-called half house — build the center bay with one side bay, which gives a house measuring 18 feet by 22 feet 8 inches overall. On the main level, a kitchen/dining/living room could occupy the 14-foot bay and the hearth, stairs, and entry could occupy the 8-foot bay. Above could be one large bedroom and a bath or two smaller bedrooms and a bath.

The only modification necessary to build a half-house frame is to lay out the smaller bay's exterior wall as an exterior bent. The sill girder on the end wall can be reduced from an 8x10 to an 8x9. The

◀ *An 18-foot by 23-foot half house.*

▲ *An 18-foot by 36-foot cape.*

plates, since they are only about 23 feet long, no longer need a scarf joint.

The half house can be added to later if necessary to create a "full" house. If you are planning that from the start, cut the necessary mortises for the add-on framing now. When you pour your foundation, leave some reinforcing steel bars protruding for the add-on and/or provide a vertical keyway.

The Cape

You could use the full first-floor plan but only make the house one full story — a good solution for someone who doesn't want to climb stairs. For more second-floor space, the roof could be steepened to provide space for two bedrooms under the roof, or the roof could take on a gambrel form to increase that space even more. Unfortunately, capes are not added to easily or gracefully. A lean-to with a low eave and shallow pitch is the easiest way. You might be surprised to find that many old capes were jacked up to add another story under them. If you find an old two-story house with a timber-framed second floor and roof but stud walls below, this

is undoubtedly what has occurred. Kneewalls (less than full-height walls above the first floor) are relatively common in modern timber frames, but they can potentially cause structural concerns. I wouldn't add them to this design without the advice of a structural engineer.

A Cabin

The ultimate shrinking of the design is to build a one-bay cape measuring 14 feet by 18 feet. This would make a great woods cabin, office, artist's studio, or workshop. It is a great beginner project! The 8x10 sill girder now becomes an exterior 8x9 sill and, of course, no scarfs are necessary in the sills or plates. This cabin could be expanded lengthwise in the future to the full 36-foot length and become the cape. Again, allow mortises for the add-on framing.

The 18-foot width of the frame can be reduced without reengineering the design. If you find that a width of 16 feet, for example, is more appropriate, you don't need to adjust any of the timber sizings or joints.

Expanding on the Plan

A big advantage of the hall-and-parlor house, especially the two-story version, is the ease of adding on building components that extend and compliment the house form. For starters, an ell (which is an addition off the side or at right angles to a building) could be added off the kitchen to provide an entry room, firewood storage, and/or garage. This ell might have an earthen floor with large flat stones and could be open to the south. A single-story ell with a roof ridge parallel with the main house would not obscure upper-story windows and if set back from

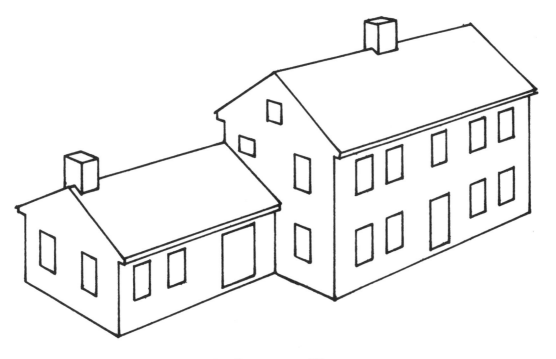

AN ELL OFF THE WEST SIDE

the front of the house a bit would still allow east light into the kitchen. The house shown in many of the photos has just such an ell. In early times, this ell contained firewood storage, work areas, and the privy in northern climates.

Another ell could be added on the west in a similar fashion to house a master bedroom suite with its own bath. Again, a single-story structure set back from the front of the house would not obstruct the upper-floor windows. A formal design is thus created by having the central mass flanked by symmetric ells.

A lean-to (or outshot, as some call them) can be added off the north wall to virtually double the first floor area. It can continue the main roof pitch straight out until an 8-foot wall is left — a "cat-slide" roof. You can create a broken-back saltbox by lessening the pitch for the lean-to. As shown in the photos, you could also drop the roof down from the main

▲ *The owners of the project house opted for a two-bay ell with a dirt floor. The framing is consistent with that of the main house but the roof pitch is 6-in-12.*

A "Cat Slide" Saltbox Roof

A Broken-Back Saltbox

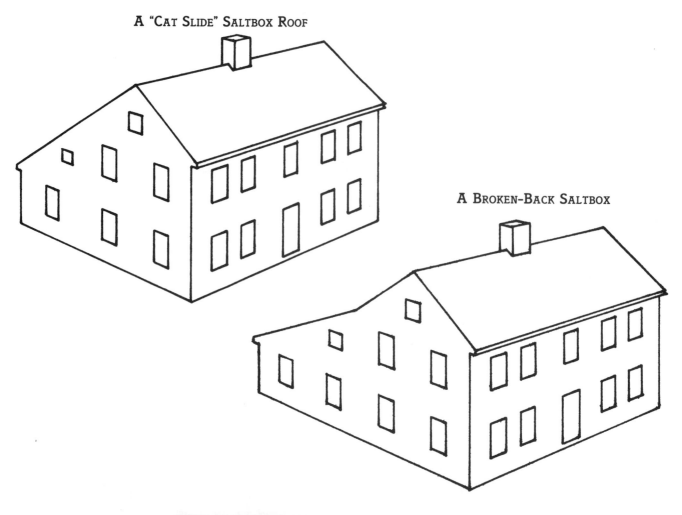

▶ *This house has a narrow two-story high lean-to creating a broken-back saltbox. Lowered interior ceilings are required for some rooms.*

roof a few feet to allow windows on the north wall of the second floor, but here the lean-to was only one bay wide and was a continuation of the ell. A greenhouse or sunroom lean-to could be added off the south side for solar heating.

One could also add a cape ell off the north wall with a ridge perpendicular to the main roof. This could provide a huge family room with extra sleeping room above or possibly an open loft. One of my favorite add-ons aesthetically is a series of progressively shorter additions starting off at one end of the main house, creating a rhythmic effect. There is a distinct advantage to adding a structure against a two-story wall: The addition's roof easily

▲ *This ell continues behind the house to become a lean-to for one bay.*

◄ *A 5-inch by 13-inch header/girt between posts supports the lean-to rafters.*

▲ *This late 1700s cape house in Adams, Massachusetts, had an early 1800s hall-and-parlor house (measuring 20 feet by 40 feet) built against it.*

▶ *This classic house in New York has telescoping additions.*

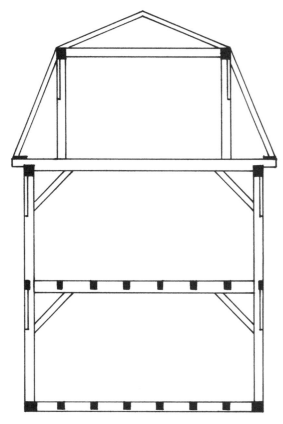

FRAMING THE HALL-AND-PARLOR GAMBREL

THE HALL-AND-PARLOR GAMBREL

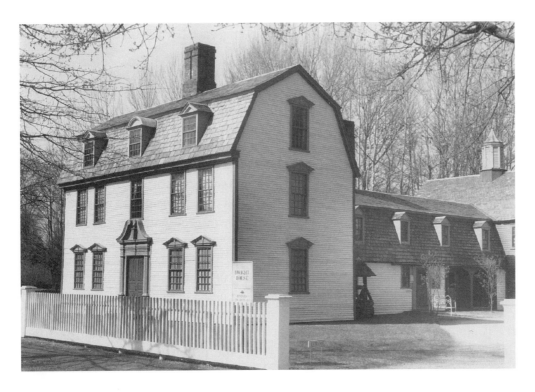

◀ *The Dwight House in Old Deerfield, Massachusetts, built around 1754, has a gambrel roof as well as an ell and an attached barn.*

▲ *This house has a wrap-around porch.*

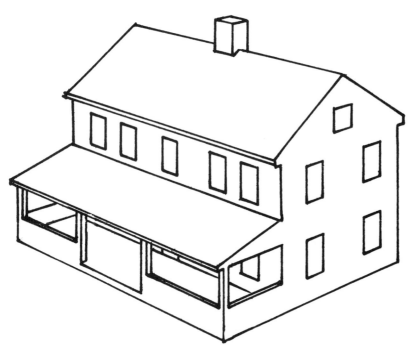

▲ *A porch add-on extends the living space in summer.*

butts against the wall rather than uncomfortably meshing against roofs or cornices. Lean-tos with only a single roof plane are easily added.

You can also go up to gain more space. In fact, another story might be the most reasonable way to go considering the addition doesn't need a foundation. The roof could easily become a gambrel shape with some dormers to provide a couple of rooms in the attic. The stairs to this new level would rise above the present stairs so as not to diminish space on the second floor. To frame a gambrel roof in timber, add a continuous purlin plate with braces on each side where the pitch changes. The purlin plates are supported by posts resting on the attic floor tie beams. Ceiling joists span between them much like the attic floor. Insulate the ceiling. Use planks nailed to the exterior side of the purlin plate for walls that are insulated just as the main house walls. A gambrel roof gives a finished room width of about 13 feet. A south-facing dormer in each bay will help light the rooms.

Porch

An important item lacking in many of today's homes is the porch. I don't mean open decks off the back of the house, but a place on the sunny side of the house with a roof and railings, a place where you can watch the world with some degree of privacy. Porches act as an extension of the living area in the warmer months and places where children can play on rainy days. They're even nice for sleeping on hot summer nights. A porch should extend out at least 7 or 8 feet, have a solid or partially open railing for privacy, and a roof with sufficient overhang to keep rain off the porch floor. In some areas a

BUILD A CLASSIC TIMBER-FRAMED HOUSE

screened porch is essential if it is to be enjoyed all summer.

All the framing and flooring should be of a rot-resistant species, and the floor should be pitched away from the house to shed water.

The Barn

In the early days, the self-sufficient farmstead required a barn to shelter the livestock, store the crops, thresh the grains, and store equipment. Although the original New England barns were detached from the house, by the 1800s builders and farmers began moving and building barns so that they were connected to the house complex — see Hubka (1984). If a barn is attached to an ell off the east end of the house, the buildings can create a south-facing enclosure that is a great outdoor work area, even in winter.

The barn size is dependent on its use, of course, but most of the old New England barns were around 30 feet by 40 feet or larger. The equilateral triangle inscribed within its cross section was the most common geometric layout principle.

Even without animals, a barn-type building is still very useful, giving a work area for large projects, such as making cider, boat building, timber framing, and repairing equipment. It is also great storage for large bulky items like vehicles, tractors, boats, ladders, lumber, furniture, and sports gear. The main floor can be earthen with a wood-floored loft above. If the barn is attached, you can walk from the house through an ell and into the barn — a very handy feature in bad weather.

▲ *Adding a barn off the ell creates a classic New England farmstead.*

No framing plans for the barn are included herein, but with the experience you have gained, it shouldn't be too hard for you to work it out. You might want to study a few barns in your area to see how they were laid out and framed, then draw up some sketches and have a structural engineer check them over. Remember that geometry makes a shape pleasing to the eye.

Where to Go from Here

I hope that this book has inspired you to build your own timber-framed house, one that stands proud and strong — a healthy house that enriches your life. If you build such a house, you will be continuing a tradition that is thousands of years old, a tradition that was nearly lost but now is strong again. Perhaps you will even go on to build for others. But, if I cannot add you to the growing list of timber-frame builders, then possibly you might become more involved in one of the associated professions. The craft needs woodland stewards who can manage our forests for sustained yields of quality products without destroying ecosystems. The craft needs more local sawyers to supply our timber needs, and tool makers that understand the old tools and how they were used. The craft also needs more architects, engineers, and building code officials that understand the principles of timber framing. And, of course, the craft needs more dedicated researchers to study the history of the craft and unlock its secrets.

Timber framing is not just a relic from the past or a curiosity. It is a viable house building technique that makes as much sense now as it ever did. I hope that you find it as rewarding as I have.

An Introduction to Structural Design

A little bit of knowledge can sometimes be a problem. For instance, if you think that with only a joist and rafter span table you can do your own structural design, you are mistaken. Though you could get by in most conventional stud-framed houses, timber-framed dwellings are less forgiving. There are no tables for members that are notched or mortised. There are no tables for joints. One reason I wrote this book is that there are few timber-framed house plans (and no other books) available for the builder without an engineering background. In the hall-and-parlor house design outlined in this book, the timbers and their joints have already been sized to meet the loads shown in the table on this page.

With the exception of the roof load, these numbers are consistent with most building codes, though you should check with your local code official. Roof loads are more variable and depend on the

Ground Floor:	40 psf (pounds per square foot) live load
Second floor:	30 psf live load
Attic floor:	30 psf live load
Roof:	40 psf live load

amount of snow or wind in your area. Again, check with your local official. The timber sizes included here are designed to meet or exceed these loadings using eastern white pine for all but the main posts and braces. Though it is one of the weakest of commercially available species, it is inexpensive and readily available in the Northeast. If you follow the framing plans, use the grades of timber specified, cut reasonably close tolerances on the joints, sheath the structure properly, and use the building as a residence (and not an anvil warehouse), your frame should stand indefinitely, barring any natural disasters.

If, on the other hand, you wish to modify the design, have larger loading requirements, or just want to understand structural design, you can follow along through the design of a couple of members. These examples should not, however, be considered a substitute for a complete engineering-level structural understanding.

A Floor Joist

The first-floor joists in our design are spaced every 2 feet 6 inches on center. Changing this spacing affects the loading on each joist. Those joists in the end bays span greater distances than those in the central bay. I have designed the joists for the larger span of the two bay types and recommended the same joist size and joinery for both spans. The span for members is usually taken as the center-to-center distance of the members supporting them. Thus, the span for the 14-foot bay is 13 feet 2 inches. The loading on a joist is the sum of the live load (from the code) and the dead load (the weight of the flooring system). On this house, a typical dead load might look like the following:

¾-inch hardwood (maple) finish floor	2.75 psf
¾-inch spruce subfloor	1.66 psf
pine floor joist	3.10 psf
(estimated size 6x7, with 7.76 pounds per foot of length for each 2.5 square feet of floor it supports)	
Total dead load	7.51 psf

I erred on the side of safety and assumed an even 10 psf dead load. Added to the live load of 40 psf, the floor load totals 50 psf. Since each joist supports 2.5 square feet of floor for every foot of its length, its loading is 125 pounds per foot of length. Next, I will demonstrate how to investigate the joist for bending, deflec-

tion, and horizontal shear. As each of these could cause problems — if not collapse — the joist must be checked for all three forms of stress.

Bending. A joist will break when the stresses in the wood exceed the allowable bending stresses. Breaks usually occur in the middle of the joist. During extreme loading, the fibers in the upper half of the joist are compressed beyond their capacity and those in the lower half are stretched (placed in tension) beyond their capacity. The fibers in the middle or neutral axis are under little or no stress; the greatest stresses occur on the top and bottom surfaces. Structural steel I-beams are shaped with more material where the greatest bending stresses occur. In technical terms, a floor joist is *simply* supported, which means it spans between two supports. Calculating the stresses of a joist is relatively easy:

M = Bending moment
L = Length of span in feet
w = uniform load per foot of span

$$M = \frac{wL^2}{8} \times 12 \text{ inches/foot}$$

$$M = \frac{(125 \text{ lbs.}) \, (13.16 \text{ ft}^2)}{8} \times 12 \text{ in/ft}$$

$$M = 32{,}472.3 \text{ inch-pounds}$$

To determine our joist size from this bending moment, plug in the bending strength value for the chosen species of wood. What value do we use? The allowable unit stresses vary with the cross-sectional size of the member. The larger the member, the lower the unit stress, which is because larger members tend to have larger checks and more hidden defects.

DIMENSIONAL LUMBER CATEGORIES

Light framing	2–4 inches thick, 2–4 inches wide
Structural joists and planks	2–4 inches thick, 5 inches or wider
Beams and stringers	5 inches or thicker, width more than 2 inches greater than thickness
Posts and timbers	5x5 or larger, width less than or equal to 2 inches more than thickness

Structural dimension lumber is divided into four categories by size (see the table above).

Each size classification has its various grades (see chart of design values for eastern white pine on page 178).

Our joist will probably fall into the joists and planks category. With #1 grade, use $Fb = 1000$, which goes into the formula:

$$S = M/Fb \quad S = 32{,}472.3/1000 = 32.47$$

M = bending moment
Fb = extreme fiber in bending from table
S = section modulus

This section modulus is a number that represents the size and cross section of a beam. If we know S, we can select timber sizes. The S required to meet the bending moment is 32.47. How large a timber is needed to meet this? To determine S for a given beam:

$$S = bd^2$$

b = width of the beam
d = the depth of the beam
The section modulus of a 4x7 is

$$\frac{(4)\,(7)^2}{6} = 32.66$$

Since this amount is slightly greater than required, this size passes the bending test.

Deflection. Now, I will check the 4x7 to see if it meets the deflection criteria. The formula for a simply supported and uniformly loaded beam is:

$$D = \frac{5Wl^3}{384\,EI}$$

$$D = \frac{5(1645)\,(158)^3}{384\,(1{,}200{,}000)\,114.33} = .616 \text{ inch}$$

D = Deflection
W = Total load on beam: $W = 125 \times 13.16 = 1645$ pounds
l = Length of span in inches: $l = 158$ inches
E = Modulus of elasticity
I = Moment of inertia of beam: the I for a rectangular beam = $\dfrac{bd^3}{12}$

I for a 4x7 = 114.33

The maximum allowable deflection is set by the building code. Though sagging floors may not be a structural problem, they can cause cracking plaster, sloping floors, and make china cabinets rattle when you walk by, as well as create a feeling of uneasiness. Thus, deflection is typically limited to $\frac{1}{360}$th of the span when considering just the live load, or $\frac{1}{240}$th of the span when considering both the live and dead loads. Since the loading in this case includes both live and dead loads already, I will use $\frac{1}{240}$. Thus, the allowable deflection is $^{158}/_{240}$ or .658 inch. Since .624 inch is less than the limit, the beam is fine.

Shear. There are two types of shear: vertical and horizontal. Vertical shear is mostly a concern in masonry work — because of the fiber structure of wood, vertical shear is not a concern for timber-framed buildings. Horizontal shear must be considered, however. A floor joist can meet the above bending and deflection requirements but still fail in horizontal

DESIGN VALUES FOR EASTERN WHITE PINE

SIZE	GRADE	F_B	F_B (REP MEM)	F_t	F_v	F_{CPERP}	F_{CPAR}	E
LIGHT FRAMING								
	Select Structural	1350	1550	800	70	350	1050	1,200,000
	#1	1150	1350	675	70	350	850	1,200,000
	#2	950	1100	550	70	350	675	1,100,000
	#3	525	600	300	70	350	400	1,000,000
	Appearance	1150	1350	675	70	350	1000	1,200,000
	Stud	525	600	300	70	350	400	1,000,000
	Construction	700	800	400	70	350	750	1,000,000
	Standard	375	450	225	70	350	625	1,000,000
	Utility	175	200	100	70	350	400	1,000,000
JOISTS AND PLANKS								
	Select Structural	1150	1350	775	70	350	950	1,200,000
	#1	1000	1150	675	70	350	850	1,200,000
	#2	825	950	425	70	350	700	1,100,000
	#3	475	550	250	70	350	450	1,000,000
	Appearance	1000	1150	675	70	350	1000	1,200,000
	Stud	475	550	250	70	350	450	1,000,000
BEAMS AND STRINGERS								
	Select Structural	1050	–	700	65	350	675	1,100,000
	#1	875	–	600	65	350	575	1,100,000
POSTS AND TIMBERS								
	Select Structural	975	–	650	65	350	725	1,100,000
	#1	800	–	525	65	350	625	1,100,000

F_B = Extreme fiber in bending, single member uses
F_B (Rep Mem) = Extreme fiber in bending, repetitive member uses
F_t = Tension parallel to the grain
F_v = Horizontal shear
F_{CPrep} = Compression perpendicular to the grain
F_{CPar} = Compression parallel to the grain
E = Modulus of elasticity

From: American Institute of Timber Construction. *Timber Construction Manual*, third edition. New York: John Wiley & Sons, Inc. 1986. Copyright © 1986, by American Institute of Timber Construction. Reprinted by permission of John Wiley & Sons, Inc.

shear. But what is horizontal shear?

Consider a beam made up of two stacked boards. When weight is applied, the boards sag and slide against each other. They slide the most at their ends and not at all in the middle of the span. Horizontal shearing, then, is this sliding action in a single beam and it, too, is greatest at the beam's ends and null in the middle of the span. Shear is a problem in timber-framed buildings when members are notched or otherwise reduced in cross section at joints. The ends of our first-floor joists must be reduced in depth where they enter the sills. Otherwise, the sills would have to be 3 or 4 inches deeper in section than the floor joist to provide wood below the joint. Since 10- or 11-inch deep sills are not practical, the joist is notched down in depth at the ends to work with an 8-inch deep sill. When a joist fails in horizontal shear at its notched end, a crack develops at the notch, though we don't actually see the two halves sliding against each other. Once the halves slide a fraction of an inch, the cohesion between the fibers is broken. The joist acts like two beams, with an unsupported lower beam and an upper beam that is not strong enough to support the load. A joist notched with a square-cornered notch tends to concentrate these shearing stresses at the corners of the notch. It is common to see failures of joists notched in this way in old structures. The best way to handle the stress is to angle the cut back at approximately 45 degrees to spread out the stresses. By removing additional wood, the joist is strengthened. It is common to see in old structures that joists cut in this way have not failed. In fact, such joists would usually break in the center of the span from bending rather than fail at the notch in shear. I

▲ *The floor joists are reduced in depth where they enter the sill to keep the sill size manageable. Avoid stress concentration there by angling the joist back from the notch.*

know of a house with approximately 8-inch diameter log joists, just flattened on the top, that were notched down to only 1½ inches deep and 6 inches wide at their ends. After 250 years, these joists have not failed.

Notching a joist at the ends does not affect either bending or deflection, just the allowable shear. I must check the shear by first determining the load on the joist end. In a uniformly loaded beam such as a floor joist, the weight on each end is half the total load on the beam, or one-half of 1645, or 822.5 pounds. There are two formulas, one for square-cornered notches and the other for tapered- or angled-corner notches. I will solve for each type.

Square-cornered notch

$$V = \frac{2Fv\, b\, d'}{3} \times \frac{d'}{d} = \frac{2(70)(4)(4)}{3} \times \frac{4}{7}$$

$$= 426.66 \text{ pounds}$$

V = Maximum allowable load (vertical shear) for this notch

Fv = Allowable horizontal shear

b = The width of the beam: 4 inches

d' = The depth of the beam above the notch: 4 inches

d = The total depth of the beam: 7 inches

A joist with a square-cornered notch is not sufficient in this case to support the loads.

Angled-corner notch

$$V = \frac{2Fv\, b\, d}{3} = \frac{2(70)(4)(4)}{3}$$

$$= 746.66 \text{ pounds}$$

In this case, d is the depth of the beam at the notch. Although this angled notch is considerably stronger, it still isn't sufficient. Since we don't want to cut notches any deeper into the sills and girders or make the sills and girders deeper, the joists need to be wider. If we try a 5x7 joist, a funny thing happens. Because the joist is 5 inches thick, it falls into the size category of posts and timbers. Using the same grade (#1), the allowable horizontal shear is now 65. The V for a 5x7 reduced to a 5x4 at the end is 866.66 pounds. Since that is greater than 826, it passes the shear test. But, since the new size changed the dimensions to the posts and timbers category, the other allowable stresses have also been reduced. The allowable bending stress (Fb) is now only 800. After determining the required section modulus again, it becomes apparent

that a 5x7 is not quite strong enough.

$$S = \frac{M}{Fb} = \frac{32,472.3}{800} = 40.59$$

S for a 5x7 is 40.83

It just squeaks by, but it is too close for comfort. If a joist were slightly undersized, there could be a problem. I prefer to use the next larger size.

S for a 6x7 is 49, which is more than sufficient to meet bending requirements. For deflection, E in the new category is also less: 1,100,000 instead of 1,200,000. But a 6x7 has a higher I value that more than makes up for the reduction in the modulus of elasticity. From the deflection formula, the actual deflection for a 6x7 is .448 inches, which is well under the maximum allowable deflection of .624 inches. The foregoing calculations show that horizontal shear is an important sizing factor for timbers reduced at their ends. It is also clear that wider, more squarish beams perform better for horizontal shear. For bending and deflection, narrower but deeper beams perform better. What we need, then, is a beam that is the best compromise between the two. Traditionally, beam cross sections varied depending on their method of conversion from the log and the use of the building. Although I discuss conversion elsewhere, I can tell you that squarish beams are easier to hew from round logs. Narrow stock like 2x8s are easy to saw out. In old barns, the floor joists are often logs hewn on the top and sometimes the bottom as well. They are wider than deep, and although these floors may sag considerably under heavy loads, they will not fail in horizontal shear or bending. Deflection was not a concern for the farmer, but ultimate strength was. In fact, the sagging was a sort of visual gauge of the floor's capacity. A stiff floor of 2x12s that is overloaded will not sag appreciably but it will fail abruptly; such a floor lacks visual clues as to its strength.

As plastered ceilings became popular in the latter parts of the eighteenth century, joists became narrower but deeper to increase the stiffness of the ceiling, which was necessary to keep the plaster from cracking. Thus, 2x8s and 2x10s became common in houses. These joists were usually notched where they entered the carrying timber (typically of the same depth as the joists) with the square-cornered variety to gain nailing for lath. They were often notched to half their depth and joists split at the notch from shear are common.

In this design, the second-floor joists need not be as heavy. The second-floor loading is less than the first's and the entire joist end can be housed into the girding beam. The girding beam is not under the same constraints as the sills and can be deeper in cross section as necessary. Although there is more work involved, fully housed joists are stronger in horizontal shear and provide a bit more finished appearance for the living space. The girding beams support the second-floor joists and are a key structural element. I will next examine how to go about sizing such a beam.

Girding Beam Design

Though there are four of these members in the second floor, I only designed for the one with the greatest loading and then made all four the same. The end wall girding beams are supported by the vertical wall planks and support only half a floor bay. I will look at one of the two center girding beams.

These beams carry half of the floor on either side, an 11-foot wide floor. In the two interior crossframes, a one-story (prick) post supports each girding beam. The brace at the other end picks up some vertical weight, though not all of it, and the span can be adjusted to reflect this. I will use 10.5 feet as the span. A beam continuous over three or more supports is stronger than a simply supported one, but since joinery reduces the cross section over the posts, think of each span as separate beams. This errs on the side of safety. The beam receives its loads only at the joist locations, and each joist carries a floor section 2.5 feet wide.

Live load:	30 psf
Dead load:	10 psf
Total load:	40 psf

At each of the loading points, the load is 2.5 feet x 11 feet x 40 psf = 1100 pounds. The load of the beam must also be added to this number. Assuming an 8x10 beam of eastern white pine and about 14 pounds per linear foot, the beam has about 35 pounds added to each loading point. To determine the bending stress, I use a different formula (from Parker and Ambrose [1984], p. 72) because the beam is loaded at three points rather than uniformly.

P = Point load: 1135 pounds

$$M = \frac{PL}{4} \times 12 \text{ inches per foot}$$

$$M = \frac{(1135)(10.5)}{4} \times 12 = 35,752.5$$

To determine the required section modulus, divide M (35,752.5) by the allowable bending stress for pine, which is 800 (#1, post and timbers). Thus, the required section modulus is 44.7. If the floor joists just sat on top of the girding beam without notching, a 6x8 timber would probably suffice. However, when a beam is notched or mortised to accept other members, the beam is weakened where wood is removed. How much wood and where exactly you remove it determines the final strength. It is important to de-termine the actual section modulus at the joist notches where the beam is weakest. The section modulus of the beam at these notches is not just the cross sectional area of the beam remaining after the notching; it is very important **where** the wood is removed. If wood is removed on the top

COMPARATIVE CROSS SECTIONS THROUGH GIRDING BEAM AT JOIST LOCATIONS

①

100%

②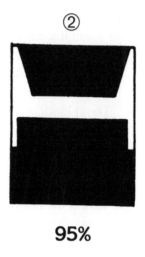

95%

③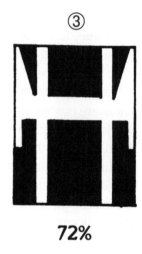

72%

④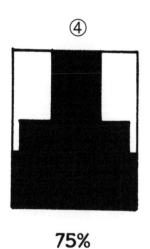

75%

⑤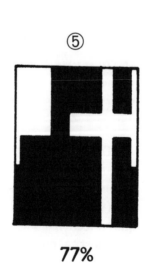

77%

⑥

66%

BUILD A CLASSIC TIMBER-FRAMED HOUSE

or bottom surfaces, the beam is weakened substantially. If it is removed from the middle near the neutral axis, it is hardly weakened at all, which is apparent from various illustrated cross sections and their resultant percentage of full strength.

Example 1 shows a full 8x10 beam without any cuts. Example 2 shows a beam with mortises cut for soffit tenons with diminished haunches. Because the wood on the top and bottom surfaces is virtually uncut, it is approximately 95 percent of full strength. It would seem that structurally this is the ideal joint for floor joists. The only drawback is that the cutting and assembly of the frame becomes a bit more time consuming. Example 3 is the same joint but with ⅞-inch peg holes for each mortise. *S* is now 72 percent of full strength, a significant change. There is an argument, though, that the wood removed by the peg hole from the upper half (compression half) is replaced by a tight-fitting peg. Example 4 has simple drop-in joist pockets and is approximately 75 percent of full strength. Example 5 is the actual section in this design in the middle of the span. It has a drop-in joist on one side and a tying joist with a peg hole on the other side. It is 77 percent of full strength. The final example has a drop-in lap dovetail on either side. Because most of the top surface is notched, it has the lowest strength, though there is more wood left than examples 3, 4, and 5; it is about 66 percent of full strength. I decided on an 8x10 notched as in example 5, giving us a section modulus of about 103, far more than the 45 required. An 8x10 is used because there should be some depth below the joist pockets and wood left between them on the top side. Using a smaller timber is not practical. Here is an example of sizing a member mostly to accommodate the joinery.

How does one figure the actual section modulus of a beam or post where it is notched? The process is a bit too involved to be included herein, but to find out more see pages 30 to 31 of *Simplified Design of Structural Wood* (Parker 1979).

Bearing. A beam can meet all the above criteria but still lack sufficient bearing area where it sits on its supports and crushing of the fibers can result. In other words, design joints with sufficient weight-bearing area on both members. First, determine the load on the joint. Then, divide the load by the allowable compression value for the particular species and grade. Use *Fc* (compression parallel to grain) for loads bearing on end grain such as a post shoulder. Use *Fc Perp* (compression perpendicular to grain) for loads bearing on side grains such as joist pockets.

There are, of course, many other timbers to size in this design as well as other loads, such as wind and earthquake loads. The above examples are provided only to demonstrate the complexity of design of a timber-framed structure. A thorough study of all the loads on the timbers and joints is beyond the scope of this book. Structural engineers are best suited to analyze timber-framed structures.

Resources

Sawmills

Canadian Board Master, Inc.
RR 2, Highway 7 West
Marmora, Ontario
Canada KOK 2MO
613-472-2122

Breezewood, Inc. (maker of
    Breezewood Bandmills)
South 4th Street, P.O. Box 266
Reynoldsville, PA 15851
814-653-9500

Kasco Portable Band Saw Mill
Kasco Mfg. Company, Inc.
170 West 600 North
Shelbyville, IN 46176
317-398-7973 or -4636

RipSaw Portable Sawmill
Better Built Corporation
845 Woburn Street
Wilmington, MA 01887
508-657-5636
(fax: 508-658-0444)

Woodcraft Portable Sawmill
19564 - 60th Avenue
Surrey, B.C.
Canada V3S 4N9
604-940-0121

Wood-Mizer
Wood-Mizer Products, Inc.
8180 West 10th Street
Indianapolis, IN 46214-2400
800-553-0182

The Mobile Dimension Saw (portable
    circular sawmills)
Mobile Manufacturing Company
798 N.W. Dunbar Avenue
P.O. Box 250
Troutdale, OR 97060
503-666-5593
(fax: 503-661-7548)

Sperber Tool Works (portable
    chainsaw mills)
P.O. Box 439
Bennington, VT 05201
802-442-8839

Tool Suppliers

Al Borneman
15 Belmont Drive
Smithtown, NY 11787
516-667-8686 or 516-543-5507
The Square Rule Layout Template (shown on p. 75) is very handy for layout work — it has a series of slots parallel to a long fence and can be used to lay out joinery in ½-inch increments.

Canadian Handcrafted Homebuilders'
    Supply
P.O. Box 940
Minden, Ontario K0M 2K0
705-286-3305
(fax: 705-286-4567)

Crosscut Saw Company
P.O. Box 7870
Seneca Falls, NY 13148
315-568-5755
Besides crosscut saws, they also carry logging and hewing tools.

Garrett Wade Company
161 Avenue of the Americas
New York, NY 10013
800-221-2942

Lee Valley Tools Ltd.
1080 Morrison Drive
Ottawa, Ontario
Canada K2H 8K7
800-267-8767 (orders)
800-267-8761 (inquiries)

Lehman Hardware and Appliances, Inc.
P.O. Box 41
Kidron, Ohio 44636
216-857-5757 or -5441
Some timber framing, hewing, and logging tools. The catalog costs $2.00 at this printing.

Woodcraft Supply
210 Wood County Industrial Park
P.O. Box 1686
Parkersburg, WV 26102-1686
800-225-1153

Hardware

Tremont Nail Company
8 Elm Street, P.O. Box 111
Wareham, MA 02571
508-295-0038
Old-style nails and hardware.

Masonry Heaters

Masonry Heater Assoc. of North America
11490 Commerce Park Drive
Reston, VA 22091
703-620-3171
This group can provide a listing of qualified masons, up-to-date information on masonry heaters, and other resources.

Tulikivi
The New Alberene Stone Company, Inc.
P.O. Box 300
Schuyler, VA 22969
804-831-2228 or 800-843-3473

Organizations

The Timber Framers Guild of North
  America
P.O. Box 1046
Keene, NH 03431
603-357-1706
*A not-for-profit organization devoted to
  the advancement of the craft of
  timber framing.*

Northeastern Lumber Manufacturers
  Association (NeLMA)
272 Tuttle Road
P.O. Box 87A
Cumberland Center, ME 04021
207-829-6901
Publishes Standard Grading Rules for
  Northeastern Lumber, *which includes
  structural design values for many
  Northeastern wood species including
  oaks, beeches, and maples.*

Glossary of Terms

Accordion lath: Thin sawn boards that are split into narrower sections and expanded on the wall to serve as a base for plaster.

Adz: A carpenter's shaping tool often used to trim high spots in framing work and to shape the ends of joists and rafters.

Anchorbeam: The large crossbeam in the H-bents of Dutch barns. It often has extended tenons with wedges.

Bay: The area between structural crossframes.

Bent: An assemblage of timber-frame components that can be put together lying flat and then reared up into position. Usually they are crossframes but occasionally they are longitudinal wall frames.

Best edge: The secondary reference face that is adjacent to the best face.

Best face: The primary reference face that will typically receive flooring and wall and roof sheathing.

Bow: A slight curve in a member after sawing or seasoning.

Brace: A diagonal timber or a temporary piece of lumber that prevents distortion in a frame.

Broadax: A wide-bladed ax used to square up timbers.

Chamfer: To bevel the edge of a timber.

Chord: The upper or lower timber in a truss.

Clapboards: Siding composed of thin, lapped, horizontal boards. Also referred to as weatherboards.

Crosscut: To cut across the wood fibers.

Crossgrain: Grain that is not running parallel with the edge of a timber. Occurs when a crooked or twisted timber is sawn into straight lumber.

Crown: A bow in a timber that is placed up in spanning members where the load will tend to straighten it.

Cruck blade: A large and usually curved or elbowed timber that serves as both post and principal rafter that rises from the floor (or nearly so) to support the ridge.

Cruck frame: A timber frame utilizing pairs of cruck blades to support its roof.

Drawboring/drawpinning: Offsetting peg holes in mortise-and-tenon joints so a tapered peg will pull the joint tight.

False plate: The plank that the common rafters sit on.

Froe: A tool for cleaving shingles, clapboards, pegs, or sections for furniture.

Gin pole: A lifting device composed of a single pole, stayed by guy lines, from which a block and tackle can be hung.

Girder: A large timber carrying a number of floor joists, often called a summer beam.

Girding beam: The large crossbeam carrying the second-floor joists and tying the posts at the second-floor level.

Girts: Traditionally, girts are horizontal, perimeter timbers that function as nailers for vertical sheathing. In our frame, they are effectively a floor joist mortised between posts. In contemporary literature, however, girts are virtually any horizontal timber at the second-floor level except joists.

Gunstock post: A post hewn or sawn to have a pronounced flair at the top to accommodate special joinery. Resembles a gun butt. Also called a jowled post.

Heartwood: The inner, nonliving part of the tree that is typically the more durable portion.

Housed mortise: A mortise recessed to bear the entire end of a tenoned member.

Joinery: The shaping of timbers where they mate to fasten or lock them.

Joist: The spanning timbers that the flooring is attached to.

Jowled post: A post that is wider at the top, usually cut from the flared butt of a tree. The flared butt stands upmost. Also called a gunstock post.

Juggling: Scoring a log at wide intervals and then splitting off the chunks between. It removes bulk wood prior to broadax work.

Lath and plaster: A traditional wall system in which plaster is applied over thin boards or, in modern times, wire mesh.

Marriage marks: Marks that determine a timber's placement in the frame.

Mortise: The cavity that accepts the tenon.

Peavy: A tool for rolling logs.

Pegs: Wood dowels used to secure timber joints, also called pins, treenails, and trunnels.

Pike pole: A long, light pole with an iron spike in the end that is used to push up bents when they are beyond the reach of the lifters.

Plate: The most important longitudinal timber in a frame. It ties the bents together at their tops and stiffens the wall plane where it meets the roof plane. Also called a wall plate.

Post and beam: A structural system whereby floor and roof loads are carried on principal timbers that may be merely stacked and fastened with hardware or may utilize timber joinery.

Prick post: A post of single-story height.

Purlin: Roof timbers spanning between principal rafters.

Purlin plate: A longitudinal continuous timber that supports common rafters

BUILD A CLASSIC TIMBER-FRAMED HOUSE

near the center of their span.

Rafter: The timbers spanning from eave to ridge to which the roof sheathing is attached.

Raising plate: Also called a false plate or raising piece. A plank laid flat on the projecting ends of attic floor joists on which common rafters bear.

Relish: The narrow bit of wood remaining between a mortise and the end of a timber. Also, the wood between a peg hole and the end of the tenon.

Rip: To saw wood along (parallel to) its fibers rather than across.

Rive: To split wood along the grain. For example, peg stock is *riven*.

Sapwood: The outer part of a tree, just under the bark, that contains the tree's food.

Scarf: To join two timbers to make a longer beam. Also, the joint used to join the timbers. There are many variations of scarf joints, such as bladed, bridled, and stop splayed.

Scoring: Removing the bulk of the waste wood from a log prior to using the broadax.

Scribe Rule: The older, more time-consuming system of layout where each timber is custom mated to its neighbors. The process requires setting out bents in a framing yard or on a floor deck.

Shakes: Separations between annular rings in a tree or timber.

Shrinkage: The reduction in size as wood dries.

Sills: Timbers that tie the bottom of the frame and distribute its weight along the foundation.

Spiral grain: When the wood fibers twist like a corkscrew.

Square Rule: A system of layout in which a smaller, perfect timber is envisioned within a rough outer timber; all joints are cut to this inner timber. Many timbers in a Square Rule frame are interchangeable.

Stop: When a chamfer ends, usually just before a joint.

Summer beam: A large timber spanning a room and supporting smaller floor joists on both sides.

Tenon: The reduced end of a timber that fits into a mortise.

Through-mortise, through-tenon: A tenon that goes completely through a timber.

Tie beam: A key horizontal timber, often at eave height, that prevents the thrust of the roof from spreading the walls apart.

Truss: A rigid assembly of timbers relying on triangulation to span distances impractical for a single member.

Vernacular architecture: Local building styles that are built using local labor and materials; these styles are directly influenced by regional culture, conditions, and climate.

Wallboard: A gypsum-based panel that has all but replaced traditional lath and plaster. Also called sheetrock.

Wane: Nature's chamfer; the rounded edges of a timber squared from an undersized log.

Further Reading

Alcock, N.W. *Cruck Construction: An Introduction and Catalogue.* Research Report
No. 42. London: The Council for British Archaeology, 1981.
   This is a scholarly study of cruck building and its origins, including a survey of over
   three thousand surviving examples.

Alexander, Christopher, et al. *A Pattern Language.* New York: Oxford University Press,
1977.
   This book is a must for those involved in designing or building for people. The authors have identified patterns of living common throughout the world that make life
   special. This book has changed the way we think about and design buildings.

American Institute of Timber Construction. *Timber Construction Manual.* New York:
John Wiley, 1985.

Benson, Tedd. *The Timber-Frame Home: Design, Construction, Finishing.* Newtown,
CT: The Taunton Press, 1988.
   One of the founders of the timber-framing revival shows how timber-framed
   homes can be brought into the twentieth century.

Bower, John. *The Healthy House.* New York: Carol Publishing Group, 1989.
   An information-packed book covering all aspects of building healthy homes.

Buchanan, Paul E. "The Eighteenth-Century Frame Houses of Tidewater Virginia." In
Building Early America, edited by Charles E. Peterson. Radnor, PA: Chilton Book
Co., 1976.
   Building Early America is a collection of essays concerning early building techniques.
   The Buchanan article illustrates a framing system similar to our project house.

Bushway, Stephen. *The New Woodburner's Handbook: A Guide to Safe, Healthy, and Efficient Woodburning.* Pownal, VT: Storey Communications, 1992.
Bushway provides some recent information on masonry heaters.

Cummings, Abbot Lowell. *The Framed Houses of Massachusetts Bay, 1625–1725.* Cambridge, MA: Harvard University Press, 1979.
This excellent book with wonderful drawings and photographs is an in-depth study of all aspects of early homes.

Dunbar, Michael. *Restoring, Tuning, and Using Classic Woodworking Tools.* New York: Sterling Publishing Co., 1989.
This book was not written with timber framers in mind, although there are worthwhile sections on evaluating and using chisels, bit braces, saws, planes, spokeshaves, and drawknives.

Fine Homebuilding. Timber-Frame Houses. Newtown, CT: The Taunton Press, 1992.
A compilation of articles on timber framing from the pages of *Fine Homebuilding.*

Fink, Daniel. *The Barns of the Genesee County, 1790–1915.* Geneseo, NY: James Brunner, Publisher, 1987.
This is a landmark study that has a wealth of information on the development and construction of barns in western New York. Barn and timber-frame enthusiasts should read this book.

Fitchen, John. *The New World Dutch Barn.* Syracuse, NY: Syracuse University Press, 1968.
This is the definitive work on this barn type.

Freidland, Edward P. *Antique Houses: Their Construction and Restoration.* New York: Dutton Studio Books, 1990.

Gamble, James Douglas. *Broad Axes.* Los Altos, CA: Tanro Co., 1986.
Discusses the history and the different styles of axes from a collector's point of view.

Glassie, Henry. "Barn Building in Otsego County." Reprint. *Geoscience and Man* V (June 10, 1974).
This is a hard-to-find scholarly study of barns.

Harris, Richard. *Discovering Timber-Framed Buildings.* United Kingdom: Shire Publications Ltd., 1978.
This fine little book is good for those interested in English joinery and framing styles.

Hewett, Cecil Alec. *English Historic Carpentry.* London and Chichester: Phillimore & Co., Ltd., 1980.
An in-depth look at the development of English timber framing through wonderful, clear perspective drawings. This book is required reading for all serious timber-frame enthusiasts.

Hoadley, R. Bruce. *Identifying Wood.* Newtown, CT: The Taunton Press, 1990.
Useful for identifying old and new wood specimens.

———. *Understanding Wood.* Newtown, CT: The Taunton Press, 1980.
Should be prerequisite reading for all workers of wood. Covers shrinkage, movement, defects, and much more in clear, easy-to-understand language.

Hubka, Thomas C. *Big House, Little House, Back House, Barn.* Hanover, NH: University Press of New England, 1984.
An excellent study of New England's connected farm buildings.

Huff, Darrell. *How to Work with Concrete and Masonry.* New York: Harper and Row, 1976.

Linnard, William. "Sweat and Sawdust: Pit-Sawing in Wales." *Folk Life: A Journal of Ethnological Studies* 20 (1981–82).
An interesting but hard-to-find booklet on hand ripsawing.

Malloff, Will. *Chainsaw Lumbermaking.* Newtown, CT: The Taunton Press, 1982.
How to build and use a chainsaw mill to cut your own lumber.

Mack, Norman, ed. *Back to Basics.* Pleasantville, NY: The Reader's Digest Association, 1981.
This book has lots of practical information about finding land and creating a self-sufficient homestead.

Miller, Warren. *Crosscut Saw Manual.* Missoula, MN: Forest Service, U.S. Department of Agriculture, Technology and Development Center, 1988.
An excellent guide to sharpening large crosscut saws.

Parker, Harry. *Simplified Design of Structural Wood.* New York: John Wiley, 1979.
This should be a primer for understanding timber engineering. It is not too technical.

Parker, Harry, and James Ambrose. *Simplified Engineering for Architects and Builders.* New York: John Wiley, 1984.

Payson, Harold H. "Sharpening Handsaws." *Fine Woodworking Magazine* 68 (Jan/Feb 1988).
Copies of this issue are available from The Taunton Press, P.O. Box 355, Newtown, CT 06470.

Pearson, David. *The Natural House Book: Creating a Healthy, Harmonious, and Ecologically Sound Home Environment.* New York: Simon & Schuster, 1989.

Phleps, Hermann. *The Craft of Log Building.* Ottawa, Ontario: Lee Valley Tools, 1982. Although it concentrates on log building in Europe, there is much information on the nature of timber. An excellent book!

Pollio, Marcus Vitruvius: *The Ten Books of Architecture.* New York: Dover Publications, 1960.

Rossnagel, W. E. *Handbook of Rigging.* New York: McGraw-Hill, 1964. This book has very handy information on rope, knots, and rigging, including the gin pole, staging, cranes, and other relevant subjects.

Shaw, Edward. *Civil Architecture.* Boston: N.p., 1830s? A good description of the Scribe Rule and Square Rule.

Siegele, H.H. *The Steel Square.* Reprint. New York: Sterling Publishing Co., 1988. This book has a wealth of information on the use of the framing square.

Sobon, Jack, and Roger Schroeder. *Timber Frame Construction.* Pownal, VT: Storey Communications, 1984. One of the first books to popularize the timber-framing revival. Provides a historical focus as well as a survey of some of the major contemporary timber framers.

Sprague, Paul E. "The Chicago Balloon Frame." In *The Technology of Historic American Buildings,* edited by H. Ward Jandl. Washington: Foundation for Preservation Technology, 1983.

Steven Winter Associates, Inc. *The Passive Solar Construction Handbook.* Emmaus, PA: Rodale Press, 1983.

Todd, S.E. *Todd's Country Homes and How to Save Money.* Hartford, CT: N.p., 1870. Some writings on the Scribe Rule and Square Rule.

U.S. Department of Agriculture. *Wood Handbook.* Washington: Government Printing Office, 1974. This book has lots of comparative facts and figures on the different species of wood, including relative strengths, shrinkages, and rot resistance.

Whiffen, Marcus. *The Eighteenth-Century Houses of Williamsburg.* Williamsburg, VA: The Colonial Williamsburg Foundation, 1987.

Thanks to Ellen Van Olst of Stichting Historisch Boerderijonderzoek for providing information about timber-framed building practices in Holland.

INDEX

(Illustrations are indicated by page numbers in *italics;* charts and tables by page numbers in **bold.**)

BUILD A CLASSIC TIMBER-FRAMED HOUSE

Gypsum plaster, 158

H

Hall, 17
Hall-and-parlor house, 8, 16–17, 38, *16–17, 34, 152*
   center bay, 23
   early, 25
   master plan of, 19
   options for, 163
   traditional geometry of, 26
Half house, *163*
Hand-hewn timbers, marking of, 77–78
Handle, ax, 64, 65
Hay, used during raising, 141
Headers, 39, *167*
Hearth, 27–28
Heartwood durability, 59
Heater, masonry, 25, 27–28, *28*
Heat
   radiant, 24, 27–28
   quality, 27
Hemlock, eastern, 51
Hewing, 62–69, *62, 68*
   area, 63
   condition of logs, 62
   juggling, 67, *67*
   layout, 66
   sawhorses, 63, *63,* 66
   tools for, 63–65
   variations, 68–69
Hickories, 51–52
Honing, 65, 82
Hook pin, 123
House planning options
   attached barn, *171*
   cabin, 164
   cape, 164, *164,* 168
   with ell, *165, 167*
   half, 163–64
   open-plan, 24, 38
   two-cube, 27, *34*
   wrap-around porch, *170*
Housing
   cutting, 78, 87
   layout on nonreference face, 108

measuring of depth, 87
sill girder, 103

I

Identification marks, 135–36, *135–36*
Inner timber, lining to, 77
Insulation
   carpenter ants and, 32, 139
   closets, 26
   walls, 153–55
Iron dogs, 63

J

Joinery
   conflicts in, 96
   history of, 9
Joints
   cutting of, 84
   English tying, 40, *40*
   girding beam mortise, 89–91
   gunstock post, 40, 44
   housed mortise, 87–88
   housing of, 89
   jowled, 40, 44
   lap dovetail, 40, 114–20, *114–20*
   mortised brace, 92–93
   in a nonreference face, 87
   peg hole in important joints, 101
   pulling tight, 132, 134
   resisting uplift, 44
   sagging of, 180
   scarfs, 121–23, *121–23*
   stub mortise, 84–87
   tolerances of, 175
   tying, 38–45, *42, 43, 114–20,* 117
Joints, versions of, 84
Joists, 34
   attic, 124–25, *124–25*
   concealed, 39
   drop in, 110, *110*
   fitting of, *144*
   installing, *141,* 147
   mortised, 39
   pockets, *106–9*
   spacing, 176

assembling tenoned, 39–40, *139–40*
   tying, 108, *108,* 111–14, *111–14*
Jowled post, 40, 44
Juggling, 67, *67*

K

Kent-style ax, *64*
Kneewall, 13

L

Lath, 158
L bead, 159
Larix laricina. See Tamarack
Layout, 73–8
   of hand-hewn timbers, 77–78
   on ends of logs, 66, *66*
   sequence, 76–77
   systems, 73–74
   3-4-5 principle of, 26
Lean-to, 165–70
Leveling with an adz, 69
Light, 26, 28–30
Liriodendron tulipifera. See Tulip tree
Loading requirements, 176
Lobby-entrance plan. *See* Hall-and-parlor house
Locust, black, 51
Log storage under water, 61
Lumber, seasoned, 60

M

Mallet, 80, *80*
Maples, 52
Marking gauge, 75
Marks, identification, *135–36*
Marriage marks, *9*
Master plan, 19–22, **21,** *22*
Masonry heaters, 27–28, *28*
Material, 3
Mechanical advantage, 149
Mice, 32, 156
Microbevel, 83
Mistakes, 136

BUILD A CLASSIC TIMBER-FRAMED HOUSE